More Monster Knits
for Little Monsters

MORE MONSTER KNITS FOR LITTLE MONSTERS
Copyright © 2014 Quantum Publishing Ltd
Photography copyright © 2014 by Kana Beisekeyev
All rights reserved. For information:
St. Martin's Press
175 Fifth Avenue
New York, N.Y. 10010.

www.stmartins.com

Library of Congress Cataloging-in-Publication Data
Available Upon Request

ISBN 978-1-250-05352-7

First U.S. Edition: January 2015

10 9 8 7 6 5 4 3 2 1

This book was conceived and produced by
Quantum Books
6 Blundell Street
London N7 9BH

QUM.PKLM

Publisher: Kerry Enzor
Project Editor: Hazel Eriksson
Editor: Cath Senker

Designer: Rosamund Saunders
Illustrator: Andrew Pinder
Technical Illustrator: Stephen Dew

Photographer: Kana Beisekeyev
Models: Valeria Khegay, Allen Khegay, Veronica
Hakhovich, Jake Kachanovsky, Damian Gangal,
Victoria Morris-Zutler, Mason R. Gallanti, Vincent C.
Gallanti, Mishelle Parker
**Project Coordinator and Translator for Nuriya
Khegay:** Dmitriy Khegay

Production Manager: Rohana Yusof

Printed in China by 1010 Printing International Ltd

Some of the materials from the techniques section
of this book previously appeared in *Monster Knits
for Little Monsters* by Nuriya Khegay;
copyright © 2013 Quantum Publishing Ltd.

More Monster Knits
for Little Monsters

20 SUPER-CUTE ANIMAL-THEMED HAT
AND MITTEN SETS TO KNIT

Nuriya Khegay

St. Martin's Griffin
New York

contents

at-a-glance project selector: 1 star is easy and 3 stars difficult

bear hugs

fantasy friends

introduction

Welcome to all who have picked up this book! Here you will find a showcase of my favorite designs for children's knitted coverall hats.

As a young mother living in New York, I realized there was a great need for warm hats for small children to protect them from the freezing cold and bitter wind. Having been trained in handicrafts by my own mother, I set about designing winter hats for my young children. I wanted them to be cozy, comfortable, and practical. And I wanted to create cute designs that would be irresistible to children. My first book, *Monster Knits for Little Monsters*, was so popular that I was asked to write another book with an array of innovative hats and mittens for little ones, and so I now present my new collection, *More Monster Knits for Little Monsters*.

All of the hats in this collection have a unique coverall design to keep your child's head, ears, and neck warm. Except for Mini Mouse, which has a neat button fastening, the neck ruff is integral to the hat. The practical pullover design ensures that your little one won't tug off their hat while you're out and about, and with a coverall hat, you don't need a scarf as well. All the garments have matching mittens—Friendly Monster and Zany Zebra have booties too. I have also included two patterns, Cuddly Koala and Little Lamb, which have matching leg warmers for extra warmth.

I've divided the projects into chapters. *Nursery Favorites* (page 8) includes some of my simpler, more straightforward patterns. In *On Safari* (page 28) you'll find a variety of original, eye-catching wild-animal designs, and a range of patterns from beginner to advanced. *Pet Loves* (page 48) includes unusual versions of our cuddly domestic friends, suitable for beginners and intermediate knitters. *Bear Hugs* (page 68) is filled with twists on the classic teddy bear, and the patterns range from intermediate to advanced. Finally, in *Fantasy Friends* (page 92) you'll find a great selection of mythical creatures and some new knitting techniques to try.

Remember to check the knitting basics section (page 116) before you begin, to familiarize yourself with the techniques needed, and I advise you to use the recommended yarn if possible. I prefer to work with very small needle sizes but this doesn't suit everyone so I have given the manufacturer's recommended sizes in this book. Just make sure to check the gauge before you begin each project, and you'll be fine. The photos accompanying the pattern show one size, so please note that stripes may fall at different points when making different sizes. Note that you'll need to be able to do some simple crochet and a little basic embroidery for many of the patterns.

I hope that you will enjoy making *More Monster Knits for Little Monsters* as much as I do, and that the projects will spark your imagination and lead you to create your own unique designs for the little monsters in your life!

Nuriya Khegay

nursery favorites

chirpy chick

This is the perfect beginner's project. It's straightforward and quick to knit, with mittens in one color, and just a little simple crocheting required to make the eyes. A cute beak gives the chirpy chick its special character.

Coverall hat and mittens

LEVEL: beginner

SIZES
6-12 months (12-24 months, 2-3 years)

Finished measurements
From "cheek to cheek" around the hat: 14½ (15, 15½)in (37 [38, 39]cm)
Mitten circumference: 5½ (6, 6) in (14 [15, 15]cm)
Mitten length: 5½ (6½, 7½)in (14 [16.5, 19]cm)

Gauge
14 sts and 19 rows = 4in (10cm) square in stockinette stitch worked with US 10 (6mm) needles
15 sts and 19 rows = 4in (10cm) square in k1, p1 rib unstretched, worked with US 10 (6mm) needles

Materials

HAT

Yarn:
Color A: 1 x 3.5oz (100g) ball (120yd/109m) Patons Classic Wool Roving Yarn, 100% pure new wool, Yellow

Small amounts:
Color B: Patons Classic Wool Roving Yarn, 100% pure new wool, Pumpkin
Color C: Patons Classic Wool Roving Yarn, 100% pure new wool, Aran
Color D: Patons Classic Wool Roving Yarn, 100% pure new wool, Black

Equipment:
- US 10 (6mm) circular needle
- A pair of US 10 (6mm) needles
- 4 x US 10 (6mm) double-pointed needles
- US H-8 (5mm) crochet hook
- Optional: Stitch marker to indicate the start of a round.
- Yarn needle

MITTENS

Yarn:
Color A: 1 x 3.5oz (100g) ball (120yd/109m) Patons Classic Wool Roving Yarn, 100% pure new wool, Yellow

Equipment:
- 4 x US 10 (6mm) double-pointed needles
- Optional: Stitch marker to indicate the start of a round.
- Yarn needle

HAT

With a US 10 (6mm) circular needle and yarn A, cast on 52 (54, 56) sts. Join to work in the round.

Rounds 1-3 (1-3, 1-3): Work k1, p1 rib.

Work in rows.

Row 4 (4, 4): K2tog, k43 (45, 47), place next 7 (7, 7) stitches on waste yarn, turn. 44 (46, 48) sts.

Row 5 (5, 5): P44 (46, 48), turn.

Rows 6-27 (6-29, 6-29): Work in stockinette stitch.

Work in short rows.

Row 28 (30, 30): K14 (14, 15), k2tog, k12 (14, 14), k2tog, turn. 42 (44, 46) sts.

Row 29 (31, 31): Sl1, p12 (14, 14), p2tog, turn. 41 (43, 45) sts.

Row 30 (32, 32): Sl1, k12 (14, 14), k2tog, turn. 40 (42, 44).

Rows 31-50 (33-52 , 33-54): Rep. the last 2 rows 10 (10, 11) times. 20 (22, 22) sts.

Row 51 (53, 55): Rep. row 29 (31, 31) once. 19 (21, 21) sts.

Row 52 (54, 56): Sl1, [p1, k1] 5 (6, 6) times, p2tog, k2tog, turn. 17 (19, 19).

Row 53 (55, 57): Sl1, [k1, p1] 5 (6, 6) times, k1, p2tog, turn. 16 (18, 18).

Row 54 (56, 58): Sl1, [p1, k1] 5 (6, 6) times, p1, k2tog, turn. 15 (17, 17).

Row 55 (57, 59): Sl1, [k1, p1] 5 (6, 6) times, k1, p2tog, turn. 14 (16, 16).

NECK RUFF

Work in the round with a US 10 (6mm) circular needle.

Row 56 (58, 60): Sl1, [p1, k1] 5 (6, 6) times, p1, k2tog, pick up and knit 12 (14, 14) stitches along edge, from waste yarn [p1, k1] 3 (3, 3) times, p1, pick up and knit 12 (14, 14) stitches along edge. 44 (50, 50) sts.

Rounds 57-65 (59-69, 61-71): Work in k1, p1 rib.

Bind off.

EYES
(make 2)

With US H-8 (5mm) crochet hook and yarn C: Ch3. Join with sl st to form ring.

Round 1: 7sc into the center of ring. Join with sl st into top of first stitch. Fasten off.

BEAK

With US 10 (6mm) double-pointed needles and yarn B, cast on 16 sts.

Round 1: Knit.

Round 2: [K2tog, k4, k2tog] twice. 12 sts.

Round 3: Knit.

Round 4: [K2tog, k2, k2tog] twice. 8 sts.

Round 5: Knit.

Round 6: [K2tog] 4 times. 4 sts.

Cut yarn, thread through remaining stitches and draw tight.

Finishing

1 Sew the eyes to the hat in the position shown.
2 With yarn D, embroider two small pupils in satin stitch.
3 Sew the beak onto the hat.
4 Weave in ends.

MITTENS
(make 2)

With US 10 (6mm) double-pointed needles and yarn A, cast on 16 (18, 18) sts.

CUFF
Rounds 1-6 (1-8, 1-8): Work k1, p1 rib.
Rounds 7-8 (9-10, 9-10): Knit.

THUMB GUSSET
Round 9 (11, 11): K7 (8, 8), m1, k2 (2, 2), m1, k7 (8, 8). 18 (20, 20) sts.
Round 10 (12, 12): Knit.
Round 11 (13, 13): K7 (8, 8), m1, k4 (4, 4), m1, k7 (8, 8). 20 (22, 22) sts.
Round 12 (14, 14): Knit.
Round 13 (15, 15): K7 (8, 8), m1, k6 (6, 6), m1, k7 (8, 8). 22 (24, 24) sts.
Round 14 (16, 16): Knit.

12-24 months and 2-3 years:
Round (17, 17): K (8, 8), m1, k (8, 8), m1, k (8, 8). (26, 26) sts.
Round (18, 18): Knit.

All sizes:
Round 15 (19, 19): K8 (9, 9), place 6 (8, 8) thumb stitches on waste yarn. Rejoin to work in the round, k8 (9, 9). 16 (18, 18) sts.

HAND
Rounds 16-25 (20-30, 20-32): Knit.
Round 26 (31, 33): [K2tog] to end of round. 8 (9, 9) sts.
Round 27 (32, 34): Knit.
Round 28 (33, 35): [K2tog] 4 (4, 4) times, k0 (1, 1). 4 (5, 5) sts.
Cut yarn, thread through remaining stitches and draw tight.

THUMB
Transfer 6 (8, 8) stitches from waste yarn onto needles. Rejoin yarn and pick up and knit 1 st in the corner where mitten meets gusset. 7 (9, 9) sts. Join to work in the round.
Rounds 1-4 (1-5, 1-5): Knit.
Round 5 (6, 6): [K2tog] 3 (4, 4) times, k1 (1, 1). 4 (5, 5) sts.
Finish as for mitten Hand.

Finishing
Weave in ends.

This pattern makes a classic pair of generous-sized children's mittens in a single color.

little lamb

This soft hat in neutral cream has an extra-warm neck ruff for the chilliest of days. The matching mittens and leg warmers, with an attractive seed-stitch pattern, will ensure your little one stays really cozy.

Coverall hat, mittens, and leg warmers

LEVEL: beginner

SIZES
6-12 months (12-24 months, 2-3 years)

Finished measurements
From "cheek to cheek" around the hat: 14½ (15, 15½)in (37 [38, 39]cm)
Mitten circumference: 5½ (6, 6) in (13.75 [15, 15]cm)
Mitten length: 5½ (6½, 7½)in (14 [16.5, 19]cm)
Leg-warmer circumference: 7 (8, 8)in (18 [20, 20]cm)
Leg-warmer length: 10 (11, 11½)in (25.5 [28, 29]cm)

Gauge
10 sts and 20 rows = 4in (10cm) square in seed stitch worked with US 10 (6mm) needles
13 sts and 20 rows = 4in (10cm) square in k1, p1 rib unstretched, worked with US 10 (6mm) needles

Materials

HAT

Yarn:
2 x 3.5oz (100g) ball (120yd/109m) Bernat Roving, 80% acrylic, 20% wool, Rice Paper

Equipment:
- US 10 (6mm) circular needle
- A pair of US 10 (6mm) needles
- Optional: Stitch marker to indicate the start of a round.
- Yarn needle

MITTENS

Yarn:
1 x 3.5oz (100g) ball (120yd/109m) Bernat Roving, 80% acrylic, 20% wool, Rice Paper

Equipment:
- 4 x US 10 (6mm) double-pointed needles
- Optional: Stitch marker to indicate the start of a round.
- Yarn needle

LEG WARMERS

Yarn:
1 x 3.5oz (100g) ball (120yd/109m) Bernat Roving, 80% acrylic, 20% wool, Rice Paper

Equipment:
- 4 x US 10 (6mm) double-pointed needles
- Optional: Stitch marker to indicate the start of a round.
- Yarn needle

HAT

With a US 10 (6mm) circular needle, cast on 50 (52, 54) sts. Join to work in the round.

Rounds 1-4 (1-4, 1-4): Work in k1, p1 rib.

Row 5 (5, 5): P1, *k1, p1* rep. from * to * 21 (22, 23) times, place next 7 (7, 7) stitches on waste yarn, turn. 43 (45, 47) sts.

Row 6 (6, 6): P1, [k1, p1] rep. to end of round. 43 (45, 47) sts.

Rows 7-27 (7-29, 7-29): Rep. row 6. 43 (45, 47) sts. Work short rows.

6-12 months and 2-3 years:

Row 28 (30): P1, [k1, p1] 6 (7) times, p2tog, [k1, p1] 6 (6) times, k1, p2tog, turn. 41 (45) sts.

Row 29 (31): Sl1, [k1, p1] 6 (6) times, k1, k2tog, turn. 40 (44) sts.

Row 30 (32): Sl1, [k1, p1] 6 (6) times, k1, p2tog, turn. 39 (43) sts.

Rows 31-52 (33-58): Rep. rows 29-30 (31-32), 11 (13) times. 17 (17) sts.

Row 53 (59): Rep. row 29 (31) once. 16 (16) sts.

Neck ruff

Work in the round.

Round 54 (60): Sl1, [k1, p1] 6 (6) times, k1, p2tog, pick up and knit 8 (10) sts along edge, from waste yarn, [k1, p1] 3 times, k1, pick up and knit 8 (10) sts along edge. 38 (42) sts.

Round 55 (61): [K1, p1] rep. to end of round. 38 (42) sts.

Round 56 (62): [P1, k1] rep. to end of round. 38 (42) sts.

Rounds 57-86 (63-92): Rep. rounds 55-56 (61-62), 15 (15) times. 38 (42) sts.

Rounds 87-94 (93-100): Work in k1, p1 rib. 38 (42) sts. Bind off.

12-24 months:

Row 30: P1, [k1, p1] 6 times, k1, p2tog, [p1, k1] 6 times, p1, p2tog, turn. 43 sts.

Row 31: Sl1, [p1, k1] 6 times, p1, k2tog, turn. 42 sts.

Row 32: Sl1, [p1, k1] 6 times, p1, p2tog, turn. 41 sts.

Rows 33-56: Rep. rows 31-32, 12 times. 17 sts.

Row 57: Rep. row 31 once. 16 sts. Work in the round.

Round 58: Sl1, [p1, k1] 6 times, p1, p2tog, pick up and knit 9 sts along edge, from waste yarn, [k1, p1] 3 times, k1, pick up and knit 9 sts along edge. 40 sts.

Round 59: [P1, k1] rep. to end of round. 40 sts.

Round 60: [K1, p1] rep. to end of round. 40 sts.

Rounds 61-88: Rep. rounds 59-60, 14 times. 40 sts.

Rounds 89-96: P1, k1 rib. 40 sts. Bind off.

EARS

With US 10 (6mm) straight needles, cast on 14 sts.

Rows 1-9: Work in garter stitch.

Row 10: K1, k2tog, k to the last 3 sts, k2tog, k1. 12 sts.

Rows 11-12: Work in garter stitch.

Row 13-24: Rep. rows 10-12, 4 times. 4 sts.

Row 25: [K2tog] twice. 2 sts.

Row 26: Knit.

Row 27: K2tog. 1 st. Bind off.

Finishing

1 Sew the ears to the hat in position (see page 15) using an invisible seam.
2 Weave in ends.

MITTENS

(make 2)

With US 10 (6mm) double-pointed needles, cast on 16 (18, 18) sts. Join to work in the round.

CUFF

Rounds 1-6 (1-8, 1-8): Work k1, p1 rib.

Round 7 (9, 9): [P1, k1] rep. to end of round.

Round 8 (10, 10): [K1, p1] rep. to end of round.

THUMB GUSSET

Round 9 (11, 11): K1 (1, 1), m1, k1 (1, 1), [p1, k1] 7 (8, 8) times. 17 (19, 19) sts.

Round 10 (12, 12): K4 (4, 4), [p1, k1] 6 (7, 7) times, p1. 17 (19, 19) sts.

Round 11 (13, 13): M1, k3 (3, 3), m1, [p1, k1] 7 (8, 8) times. 19 (21, 21) sts.

Round 12 (14, 14): K6 (6, 6), [p1, k1] 6 (7, 7) times, p1. 19 (21, 21) sts.

Round 13 (15, 15): M1, k5 (5, 5), m1, [p1, k1] 7 (8, 8) times. 21 (23, 23) sts.

Round 14 (16, 16): K8 (8, 8), [p1, k1] 6 (7, 7) times, p1. 21 (23, 23) sts.

Round 15 (17, 17): M1, k7 (7, 7), m1, [p1, k1] 7 (8, 8) times. 23 (25, 25) sts.

12-24 months and 2-3 years:

Round (18, 18): K (10, 10), [p1, k1] (7, 7) times, p1. (25, 25) sts.

Round (19, 19): M1, k (9, 9), m1, [p1, k1] (8, 8) times. (27, 27) sts.

All sizes:
Round 16 (20, 20): K1 (1, 1), place 7 (9, 9) thumb stitches on waste yarn. Rejoin to work in the round, [p1, k1] 7 (8, 8) times, p1. 16 (18, 18) sts.

HAND
Round 17 (21, 21): [P1, k1] to end of round.
Round 18 (22, 22): [K1, p1] to end of round.
Rounds 19-23 (23-30, 23-32): Work in stockinette stitch.
Round 24 (31, 33): [K2tog] to end of round. 8 (9, 9) sts.
Round 25 (32, 34): Knit.
Round 26 (33, 35): [K2tog] 4 (4, 4) times, K0 (1, 1). 4 (5, 5) sts. Cut yarn, thread through remaining stitches and draw tight.

THUMB
Place 7 (9, 9) stitches from waste yarn onto needles. Rejoin yarn and pick up one extra stitch in the corner where mitten meets gusset. 8 (10, 10) sts. Join to work in the round.
Rounds 1-3 (1-4, 1-5): Work in stockinette stitch.
Round 4 (5, 6): [K2tog] to end of round. 4 (5, 5) sts.
Finish as for mitten Hand.

Finishing
1   Weave in ends.

LEG WARMERS
(make 2)
With US 10 (6mm) double-pointed needles, cast on 20 (22, 22) sts. Join to work in the round.

CUFF
Rounds 1-6 (1-7, 1-7): Work k1, p1 rib.
LEG
Round 7 (8, 8): [P1, k1] to end of round.
Round 8 (9, 9): [K1, p1] to end of round.
Rounds 9-34 (10-47, 10-51): Rep. last 2 rounds. 13 (19, 21) times.

CUFF
Rounds 35-39 (48-53, 52-57): P1, k1 rib.
Bind off.

Finishing
1   Weave in ends.

The mittens and leg warmers are both knitted using seed stitch—for more details, see page 131.

buzzy bee

Everyone loves bees, and this bee hat is full of character with its antennae and pompom trimmings. It has simple crochet spirals for the eyes and nose. The mittens are made in a matching striped pattern.

Coverall hat and mittens

LEVEL: beginner

SIZES
6-12 months (12-24 months, 2-3 years)

Finished measurements
From "cheek to cheek" around the hat: 14 (14½, 15)in (36 [37, 38]cm)
Mitten circumference: 5½ (6, 6½)in (13.75 [15, 16.25]cm)
Mitten length: 5½ (6½, 7)in (14 [16.5, 18]cm)

Gauge
17 sts and 23 rows = 4in (10cm) square in stockinette stitch worked with US 8 (5mm) needles
21 sts and 23 rows = 4in (10cm) square in k1, p1 rib unstretched, worked with US 8 (5mm) needles

Materials

HAT

Yarn:
Color A: 1 x 3.5oz (100g) ball (170yd/156m) Lion Brand, Vanna's Choice Baby Yarn, 100% acrylic, Black
Color B: 1 x 3.5oz (100g) ball (170yd/156m) Lion Brand, Vanna's Choice Baby Yarn, 100% acrylic, Duckie

Small amounts:
Color C: Lion Brand, Vanna's Choice Yarn, 100% acrylic, White
Color D: Lion Brand, Vanna's Choice Yarn, 100% acrylic, Scarlet

Equipment:
- 1 pair of US 8 (5mm) needles
- US 8 (5mm) circular needles
- 4 x US 5 (3.75mm) double-pointed needles
- US H-8 (5mm) crochet hook
- Optional: Stitch marker to indicate the start of a round.
- Yarn needle
- Two circles of cardboard 1in (2.5cm) in diameter or a pompom maker
- Small amount of stuffing (optional)

MITTENS

Yarn:
Color A: 1 x 3.5oz (100g) ball (170yd/156m) Lion Brand, Vanna's Choice Baby Yarn, 100% acrylic, Black
Color B: 1 x 3.5oz (100g) ball (170yd/156m) Lion Brand, Vanna's Choice Baby Yarn, 100% acrylic, Duckie

Equipment:
- 4 x US 8 (5mm) double-pointed needles
- Optional: Stitch marker to indicate the start of a round.
- Yarn needle

This side view indicates the neat join between the hat and neck ruff.

Notes:
STRIPE PATTERN REPEAT
Work in stockinette stitch, each stripe starting with a k row or round.

Rows or rounds 1-7 (1-7, 1-7): Yarn B. 8 (8, 8) rows or rounds.

Rows or rounds 8-13 (8-13, 8-15): Yarn A. 6 (6, 8) rows or rounds. Repeat the last 14 (14, 16) rows or rounds.

The photograph shows the stripe pattern as it will appear on the 6-12 month size. The shaping on other sizes will occur on different rows or rounds of the repeat.

HAT
With US 8 (5mm) straight needles and yarn A, cast on 61 (64, 67) sts.

Rows 1-6 (1-6, 1-6): Work k1, p1 rib. Join in yarn B.

Continue to work the hat pattern, while at the same time, working the Stripe pattern repeat, starting with row 1. Do not break yarns, but carry yarns up as you knit.

Rows 7-34 (7-34, 7-38): Work in Stripe pattern repeat.

Work short rows.

Continue using yarn A only, weaving yarn B across the back of the first stitches of Row 35 (35, 39).

Row 35 (35, 39): Using yarn A K19 (20, 21), using yarn B, k2tog, k19 (20, 21), k2tog, turn. 59 (62, 65) sts.

Continue working Stripe pattern repeat, starting with row 2 of repeat.

Row 36 (36, 40): Sl1, p19 (20, 21), p2tog, turn. 58 (61, 64) sts.

Row 37 (37, 41): Sl1, k19 (20, 21), k2tog, turn. 57 (60, 63) sts.

Rows 38-69 (38-71, 42-77): Rep. the last 2 rows 16 (17, 18) times. 25, (26, 27) sts.

Row 70 (72, 78): Rep. row 36 (36, 40) once. 24 (25, 26) sts.

Continue using yarn B only, carrying yarn A up as you knit.

Row 71 (73, 79): Rep. row 37 (37, 41) once. 23 (24, 25) sts.

Row 72 (74, 80): Rep. row 36 (36, 40) once. 22 (23, 24) sts.

NECK RUFF

Work in the round with a US 8 (5mm) circular needle.

Continue working Stripe pattern repeat, starting with round 8 (8, 8) of repeat.

Round 73 (75, 81): Sl1, k19 (20, 21), k2tog, pick up and knit 13 (13, 14) stitches along edge, cast on 6 (7, 6) stitches, pick up and knit 13 (13, 14) stitches along edge. 53 (55, 57) sts.

Rounds 74–88 (76–90, 82–98): Knit.

Round 89 (91, 99): *K6 (6, 6), m1* rep. from * to * 8 (8, 8) times, k5 (7, 9), m1. 62 (64, 66) sts.

Round 90 (92, 100): Knit.

Round 91 (93, 101): K3 (3, 3), m1, *k7 (7, 7), m1* rep. from * to * 8 (8, 8) times, k3 (5, 7). 71 (73, 75) sts.

Round 92–93 (94–95, 102–105): Knit.

Round 94 (96, 106): *K8 (8, 8), m1* rep. from * to * 8 (8, 8) times, k7 (9, 11), m1. 80 (82, 84) sts.

Round 95 (97, 107): Knit.

Round 96 (98, 108): K4 (4, 4), m1, *k9 (9, 9), m1* rep. from * to * 8 (8, 8) times, k4 (6, 8). 89 (91, 93) sts.

Round 97 (99, 109): Knit.

Round 98 (100, 110): *k10 (10, 10), m1* rep. from * to * 8 (8, 8) times, k9 (11, 13), m1. 98 (100, 102) sts.

Round 99 (101, 111): Knit.

Round 100 (102, 112): K16 (16, 16), m1, *k11 (11, 11), m1* rep. from * to * 7 (7, 7) times, k5 (7, 9). 106 (108, 110) sts.

Round 101 (103, 113): Knit.

Rounds 102–107 (104–109, 114–119): Work k1, p1 rib.
Bind off.

ANTENNAE
(make 2)

With US 5 (3.75mm) double-pointed needles and yarn A, cast on 6 sts. Join to work in the round.

Rounds 1–10: Knit.

Cut yarn, thread through remaining stitches and draw tight.

POMPOMS

Using two circles of cardboard 1in (2.5cm) in diameter or a pompom maker and yarn B, make 2 pompoms.

The stripes run vertically at the front of the hat, and horizontally at the back. The antennae are positioned in the center of the hat.

EYES
(make 2)

With the H-8 (5mm) crochet hook and yarn C, ch4. Join with sl st to form ring.

This pattern is crocheted in a spiral. Don't join at the end of a row but continue working.

Round 1: 7sc into the center of ring.

Round 2: 2sc into each sc. 14sc.

Round 3: 1sc into each sc. 14sc

Round 4: 1sc into each sc. 14sc

End with sl st in next st to join. Fasten off.

NOSE

With the H-8 (5mm) crochet hook and yarn D, ch4. Join with sl st to form ring.

Work as for Eyes.

Finishing

1 Tuck the loose yarn ends into the dome of the nose, and add a tiny bit of stuffing if you want.
2 Sew the nose onto the hat.
3 Using yarn A, embroider two small pupils in satin stitch, one for each eye.
4 Tuck the loose yarn ends into the dome of the eyes, and add a tiny bit of stuffing if you want.
5 Sew the eyes onto the hat.
6 Lightly stuff the antennae.
7 Sew the pompoms onto the antennae.
8 Sew the antennae onto the hat.
9 Weave in ends.

MITTENS
(make 2)

With US 8 (5mm) double-pointed needles and yarn A, cast on 24 (26, 28) sts. Join to work in the round.

CUFF

Rounds 1-10 (1-12, 1-14): Work k1, p1 rib.

THUMB GUSSET

Join in yarn B. Do not break yarn A, but carry yarns up as you knit.

Rounds 1-5 (1-5, 1-5): Yarn B, Knit.

The antennae are lightly stuffed so they stick up at the correct angle.

Right mitten:

Round 6 (6, 6): Yarn A, place first 4 stitches onto waste yarn, cast on 4 stitches (right-hand needle), join to work in the round, k20 (22, 24). 24 (26, 28) sts.

Left mitten:

Round 6 (6, 6): Yarn A, k8 (9, 10), place next 4 stitches onto waste yarn, cast on 4 stitches (right hand needle), join to work in the round, k12 (13, 14). 24 (26, 28) sts.

Right and left mittens:

Rounds 7-10 (7-10, 7-10): Yarn A, knit.

Rounds 11-15 (11-15, 11-15): Yarn B, knit.

Rounds 16-20 (16-20, 16-20): Yarn A, knit.

Rounds 21-22 (21-25, 21-25): Yarn B, knit.

Fasten off yarn B. Continue using yarn A only.

HAND

6-12 months:

Round 23: [K2tog] to end of round. 12 sts.

Round 24: Knit.

Round 25: [K2tog] to end of round. 6 sts.

12-24 months, 2-3 years:

Rounds (26-27, 26-28): Knit.

Round (28, 29): [K2tog] to end of round. (13, 14) sts.

Round (29, 30): Knit.

Round (30, 31): [K2tog] (6, 7) times, k (1, 0). (7, 7) sts.

Cut yarn, thread through remaining stitches and draw tight.

THUMB

Place 4 stitches from waste yarn onto needles. Rejoin yarn A, pick up 4 sts across the 4 cast-on sts. 8 (8, 8) sts.

Join to work in the round.

Rounds 1-6 (1-7, 1-7): Knit.

Round 7 (8, 8): [K2tog] to end of round. 4 (4, 4) sts.

Finish as for mitten Hand.

Finishing

1   Weave in ends.

The right and left mittens are knitted slightly differently for a more comfortable fit.

crazy caterpillar

This striking pink and purple hat with its playful antennae and matching mittens is sure to prove a favorite. The eyes and eye edgings are easily crocheted in rounds, and the antennae are lightly stuffed to stick up straight.

Materials

Coverall hat and mittens

LEVEL: beginner

SIZES
6-12 months (12-24 months, 2-3 years)

Finished measurements
From "cheek to cheek" around the hat: 14½ (15, 15½)in (37 [38, 39]cm)
Mitten circumference: 5½ (6, 6½)in (13.75 [15, 16.25]cm)
Mitten length: 5½ (6½, 7)in (14 [16.5, 18]cm)

Gauge
17 sts and 24 rows = 4in (10cm) square in stockinette stitch worked with US 8 (5mm) needles
19 sts and 24 rows = 4in (10cm) square in k1, p1 rib unstretched, worked with US 8 (5mm) needles

HAT

Yarn:
Color A: 1 x 3oz (85g) ball (135yd/123m) Lion Brand Jiffy Yarn, 100% acrylic, Shocking Pink
Color B: 1 x 3oz (85g) ball (135yd/123m) Lion Brand Jiffy Yarn, 100% acrylic, Violet

Small amounts:
Color C: Lion Brand Jiffy Yarn, 100% acrylic, Light Pink
Color D: Lion Brand Jiffy Yarn, 100% acrylic, Apple Green

Equipment:
• 1 pair of US 8 (5mm) needles
• US 8 (5mm) circular needles
• 4 x US US 5 (3.75mm) double-pointed needles
• US G-6 (4.25mm) crochet hook
• Optional: Stitch marker to indicate the start of a round.
• Yarn needle

MITTENS

Yarn:
Color A: 1 x 3oz (85g) ball (135yd/123m) Lion Brand Jiffy Yarn, 100% acrylic, Shocking Pink
Color B: 1 x 3oz (85g) ball (135yd/123m) Lion Brand Jiffy Yarn, 100% acrylic, Violet

Equipment:
• 4 x US 8 (5mm) double-pointed needles
• Optional: Stitch marker to indicate the start of a round.
• Yarn needle

HAT

With US 8 (5mm) straight needles and yarn A, cast on 57 (61, 65) sts.
Rows 1-6 (1-6, 1-6): Work k1, p1 rib.
Rows 7-30 (7-30, 7-32): Work in stockinette stitch, starting with a k row.
Work short rows.
Row 31 (31, 33): K18 (19, 21), k2tog, k17 (19, 19), k2tog, turn. 55 (59, 63) sts.
Row 32 (32, 34): Sl1, p17 (19, 19), p2tog, turn. 54 (58, 62) sts.
Row 33 (33, 35): Sl1, k17 (19, 19), k2tog, turn. 53 (57, 61) sts.
Rows 34-53 (34-55, 36-61): Rep. last 2 rows, 10 (11, 13) times. 33 (35, 35) sts.
Row 54 (56, 62): Rep. row 32 (32, 34) once. 32 (34, 34) sts.
Row 55 (57, 63): Sl1, [p1, k1] 8 (9, 9) times, p1, k2tog, turn, (19 (21, 21) sts worked). 31 (33, 33) sts.
Row 56 (58, 64): Sl1, [k1, p1] 8 (9, 9) times, k1, p2tog, turn. 30 (32, 32) sts.
Rows 57-66 (59-68, 65-74): Rep. last 2 rows, 5 (5, 5) times. 20 (22, 22) sts.

NECK RUFF

Work in the round with a US 8 (5mm) circular needle and yarn B.
Round 67 (69, 75): Sl1, [k1, p1] 8 (9, 9) times, p1, k2tog, pick up 13 (12, 12) sts along edge, cast on 7 sts, pick up 13 (12, 12) sts along edge. 52 (52, 52) sts.
Rounds 68-77 (70-81, 76-89): Work k1, p1 rib.
Round 78 (82, 90): K2 (3, 3), *yo, k2, yo, k11* rep. from * to * 3 times, yo, k2, yo, k9 (8, 8). 60 (60, 60) sts.

Round 79 (83, 91): K3 (4, 4), *yo, k2, yo, k13* rep. from * to * 3 times, yo, k2, yo, k10 (9, 9). 68 (68, 68) sts.
Round 80 (84, 92): K4 (5, 5), *yo, k2, yo, k15 (15, 15) * rep. from * to * 3 times, yo, k2, yo, k11 (10, 10). 76 (76, 76) sts.
Round 81 (85, 93): K5 (6, 6), *yo, k2, yo, k17 (17, 17) * rep. from * to * 3 times, yo, k2, yo, k12 (11, 11). 84 (84, 84) sts.
Round 82 (86, 94): K6 (7, 7), *yo, k2, yo, k19 (19, 19) * rep. from * to * 3 times, yo, k2, yo, k13 (12, 12). 92 (92, 92) sts.
Round 83 (87, 95): K7 (8, 8), *yo, k2, yo, k21 (21, 21) * rep. from * to * 3 times, yo, k2, yo, k14 (13, 13). 100 (100, 100) sts.

12-24 months, 2-3 years:

Round (88, 96): K (9, 9), *yo, k2, yo, k (23, 23) * rep. from * to * 3 times, yo, k2, yo, k (14, 14). (108, 108) sts.
Round (89, 97): K (10, 10), *yo, k2, yo, k (25, 25) * rep. from * to * 3 times, yo, k2, yo, k (15, 15). (116, 116) sts.

2-3 years:

Round (98): K11, *yo, k2, yo, k27 * rep. from * to * 3 times, yo, k2, yo, k16. 124 sts.
Round (99): K12, *yo, k2, yo, k29 * rep. from * to * 3 times, yo, k2, yo, k17. (132) sts.

All sizes:

Rounds 84-89 (90-95, 100-105): Work k1, p1 rib.
Bind off.

EYES
(make 2)

With US G-6 (4.25mm) crochet hook and yarn D: Ch3. Join with sl st to form ring.
Round 1: Ch2, into the center of ring work [3hdc, 3dc, 3hdc, 3dc]. Join with sl st on top of beg-ch. Fasten off.

Eye edging
(make 2)

With US G-6 (4.25mm) crochet hook and yarn C: Ch4. Join with sl st to form ring.
Round 1: Ch3, work into the center of ring [4dc, 4tr, 4dc, 4tr]. Join with sl st on top of beg-ch. Fasten off.

ANTENNAE
(make 2)

With US 5 (3.75mm) double-pointed needles and yarn B, cast on 6 sts. Join to work in the round.
Rounds 1-15: Knit.
Cut yarn, thread through remaining stitches and draw tight.

Finishing

1 Sew the eyes to the eye edging.
2 Sew the eyes to the hat in the position shown using an invisible seam.
3 Lightly stuff the antennae.
4 Sew the antennae to the hat in the position shown using an invisible seam.
5 Weave in ends.

MITTENS
(make 2)
With US 8 (5mm) double-pointed needles and yarn A, cast on 22 (24, 26) sts. Join to work in the round.

CUFF
Rounds 1-10 (1-12, 1-14): Work k1, p1 rib.

THUMB GUSSET
Fasten off yarn A. Join in yarn B.
Round 11 (13, 15): M1, knit to end of round. 23 (25, 27) sts.
Round 12 (14, 16): Knit.
Round 13 (15, 17): M1, k3, m1, k20 (22, 24). 25 (27, 29) sts.
Round 14 (16, 18): Knit.
Round 15 (17, 19): M1, k5, m1, k20 (22, 24). 27 (29, 31) sts.
Round 16 (18, 20): Knit.
Round 17 (19, 21): M1, k7, m1, k20 (22, 24). 29 (31, 33) sts.
Round 18 (20, 22): Knit.

12-24 months and 2-3 years:
Round (21, 23): M1, k9, m1, k (22, 24). (33, 35) sts.

All sizes
Round 19 (22, 24): K1, place 7 (9, 9) thumb stitches on waste yarn. Rejoin to work in the round, k21 (23, 25). 22 (24, 26) sts.

HAND
Rounds 10-32 (23-38, 25-42): Knit.
Round 33 (39, 43): [K2tog] to end of round. 11 (12, 13) sts.
Round 34 (40, 44): Knit.
Round 35 (41, 45): [K2tog] 5 (6, 6) times, k1 (0, 1). 6 (6, 7) sts.
Cut yarn, thread through remaining stitches and draw tight.

THUMB
Place 7 (9, 9) stitches from waste yarn onto needles. Rejoin yarn B and pick up one extra stitch in the corner where the mitten meets the gusset. 8 (10, 10) sts.
Rounds 1-6 (1-6, 1-8): Knit.
Round 7 (7, 9): [K2tog] to end of round. 4 (5, 5) sts.
Finish as for mitten Hand.

Finishing
1 Weave in ends.

The mittens are knitted in a straightforward two-color combination.

on safari

tiny tiger

The stripes on this adorable tiger cub hat and mittens are knitted separately so you don't need to change colors while you're working. This project is bound to be a roaring success with your little cub!

Coverall hat and mittens

LEVEL: beginner

SIZES
6-12 months (12-24 months, 2-3 years)

Finished measurements
From "cheek to cheek" around the hat: 14½ (15, 15½)in (37 [38, 39]cm)
Mitten circumference: 5½ (6, 6) in (14 [15, 15]cm)
Mitten length: 5½ (6½, 7½)in (14 [16.5, 19]cm)

Gauge
14 sts and 19 rows = 4in (10cm) square in stockinette stitch worked with US 10 (6mm) needles
15 sts and 19 rows = 4 in (10cm) square in k1, p1 rib worked with US 10 (6mm) needles, unstretched

Materials

HAT

Yarn:
Color A: 1 x 3.5oz (100g) ball (120yd/109m) Patons Classic Wool Roving Yarn, 100% pure new wool, Pumpkin

Small amount:
Color B: Patons Shetland Chunky Yarn, 75% acrylic, 25% wool, Black

Equipment:
- US 10 (6mm) circular needle
- A pair of US 10 (6mm) needles
- A pair of US 8 (5mm) needles
- Optional: Stitch marker to indicate the start of a round
- Yarn needle

MITTENS

Yarn:
Color A: 1 x 3.5oz (100g) ball (120yd/109m) Patons Classic Wool Roving Yarn, 100% pure new wool, Pumpkin

Small amount:
Color B: Patons Shetland Chunky Yarn, 75% acrylic, 25% wool, Black

Equipment:
- 4 x US 10 (6mm) double-pointed needles
- Optional: Stitch marker to indicate the start of a round
- Yarn needle

Make sure you space the stripes evenly across the hat, including one positioned between the ears.

HAT

With a US 10 (6mm) circular needle and yarn A, cast on 52 (54, 56) sts. Join to work in the round.
Rounds 1-3 (1-3, 1-3): Work in k1, p1 rib.
Work in rows.
Row 4 (4, 4): K2tog, k43 (45, 47), place next 7 (7, 7) stitches on waste yarn, turn. 44 (46, 48) sts.
Row 5 (5, 5): P44 (46, 48), turn.
Rows 6-27 (6-29, 6-29): Work in stockinette stitch.
Work short rows.
Row 28 (30, 30): K14 (14, 15), k2tog, k12 (14, 14), k2tog, turn. 42 (44, 46) sts.
Row 29 (31, 31): Sl1, p12 (14, 14), p2tog, turn. 41 (43, 45) sts.
Row 30 (32, 32): Sl1, k12 (14, 14), k2tog, turn. 40 (42, 44) sts.
Rows 31-50 (33-52, 33-54): Rep. last 2 rows, 10 (10, 11) times. 20 (22, 22) sts.

Row 51 (53, 55) Rep. row 29 (31, 31) once. 19 (21, 21) sts.
Row 52 (54, 56): Sl1, [p1, k1] 5 (6, 6) times, p2tog, k2tog, turn. 17 (19, 19) sts.
Row 53 (55, 57): Sl1, [k1, p1] 5 (6, 6) times, k1, p2tog, turn. 16 (18, 18) sts.
Row 54 (56, 58): Sl1, [p1, k1] 5 (6, 6) times, p1, k2tog, turn. 15 (17, 17).
Row 55 (57, 59): Sl1, [k1, p1] 5 (6, 6) times, k1, p2tog, turn. 14 (16, 16) sts.

NECK RUFF
Work in the round with a US 10 (6mm) circular needle.
Row 56 (58, 60): Sl1, [p1, k1] 5 (6, 6) times, p1, k2tog, pick up and knit along edge 12 (14, 14) stitches, from waste yarn [p1, k1] 3 (3, 3) times, p1, pick up and knit 12 (14, 14) stitches along edge. 44 (50, 50) sts.
Rounds 57-65 (59-69, 61-71): Work in k1, p1 rib.
Bind off.

EARS
(make 2)
With US 10 (6mm) straight needles and yarn B, cast on 19 sts.
Fasten off yarn B. Join in yarn A.
Rows 1-5: Work in k1, p1 rib.
Cut yarn, thread through remaining stitches, and draw tight.

STRIPES
(make 9)
With US 8 (5mm) straight needles and yarn B, cast on 16 sts.
Work short rows.
Row 1: K12, turn.
Row 2: Sl1, k7, turn.
Row 3: Sl1, k11.
Bind off.

Finishing

1 Sew the ears to the hat in the position shown opposite.
2 Sew the stripes to the hat using an invisible seam.
3 Weave in ends.

MITTENS
(make 2)

With US 10 (6mm) double-pointed needles and A, cast on 16 (18, 18) sts.

CUFF
Rounds 1-6 (1-8, 1-8): Work in k1, p1 rib.
Rounds 7-8 (9-10, 9-10): Knit.

THUMB GUSSET
Round 9 (11, 11): K7 (8, 8), m1, k2 (2, 2), m1, k7 (8, 8). 18 (20, 20) sts.
Round 10 (12, 12): Knit.
Round 11 (13, 13): K7 (8, 8), m1, k4 (4, 4), m1, k7 (8, 8). 20 (22, 22) sts.
Round 12 (14, 14): Knit.
Round 13 (15, 15): K7 (8, 8), m1, k6 (6, 6), m1, k7 (8, 8). 22 (24, 24) sts.
Round 14 (16, 16): Knit.

12-24 months, 2-3 years:
Round (17, 17): K (8, 8), m1, k (8, 8), m1, k (8, 8). (26, 26) sts.
Round (18, 18): Knit.

All sizes:
Round 15 (19, 19): K8 (9, 9), place 6 (8, 8) thumb stitches on waste yarn. Rejoin to work hand stitches in the round, k8 (9, 9). 16 (18, 18) sts.

HAND
Rounds 16-25 (20-30, 20-32): Knit.
Round 26 (31, 33): [K2tog] to end of round. 8 (9, 9) sts.
Round 27 (32, 34): Knit.
Round 28 (33, 35): [K2tog] 4 (4, 4) times, K0 (1, 1). 4 (5, 5) sts.
Cut yarn, thread through remaining stitches, and draw tight.

THUMB
Transfer 6 (8, 8) stitches from waste yarn onto needles. Rejoin yarn and pick up and knit 1st in the corner where mitten meets gusset. 7 (9, 9) sts. Join to work in the round.

Rounds 1-4 (1-5, 1-5): Knit.
Round 5 (6, 6): [K2tog] 3 (4, 4) times, k1 (1, 1). 4 (5, 5) sts.
Finish as for mitten Hand.

STRIPES
(make 6)
With US 8 (5mm) straight needles and yarn B, cast on 16 sts.
Work short rows.
Row 1: K9, turn.
Row 2: Sl1, k4, turn.
Row 3: Sl1, k8, turn.
Bind off.

Finishing
1 Sew the stripes onto the mittens using an invisible seam.
2 Weave in ends.

Position the stripes on the side of the mittens, as indicated here.

mischievous monkey

Your little monkey will love this hat, knitted in beautifully soft brown chenille yarn. It requires just a little simple crocheting to make the inner ears. The extra-soft mittens are guaranteed to keep little paws warm.

Coverall hat and mittens

LEVEL: beginner

SIZES
6-12 months (12-24 months, 2-3 years)

Finished measurements
From "cheek to cheek" around the hat: 14½ (15, 15½)in (37 [38, 39]cm)
Mitten circumference: 5½ (6½, 7½)in (14 [16.5, 19]cm)
Mitten length: 5½ (6½, 7½)in (14 [16.5, 19]cm)

Gauge
10 sts and 20 rows = 4in (10cm) square in stockinette stitch worked with US 9 (5.5mm) needles with yarn A
13 sts and 20 rows = 4in (10cm) square in k1, p1 rib worked with US 10 (6mm) needles with yarn B, unstretched

Materials

HAT

Yarn:
Color A: 1 x 2.5oz (70g) ball (100yd/91m) Lion Brand, Chenille Yarn, 75% acrylic, 18% poly, 7% nylon, Brownstone.

Small amount:
Color B: Bernat Roving Yarn, 80% acrylic, 20% wool, Squashed.

Equipment:
- US 10 (6mm) circular needle
- A pair of US 9 (5.5mm) needles
- US 9 (5.5mm) circular needle
- US J-10 (6mm) crochet hook
- Optional: Stitch marker to indicate the start of a round
- Yarn needle

MITTENS

Yarn:
Color A: 1 x 2.5oz (70g) ball (100yd/91m) Lion Brand, Chenille Yarn, 75% acrylic, 18% poly, 7% nylon, Brownstone

Small amount:
Color B: Bernat Roving Yarn, 80% acrylic, 20% wool, Squashed

Equipment:
- 4 x US 9 (5.5mm) double-pointed needles
- 4 x US 10 (6mm) double-pointed needles
- Optional: Stitch marker to indicate the start of a round
- Yarn needle

HAT

With a US 10 (6mm) circular needle and yarn B, cast on 52 (54, 56) sts. Join to work in the round.

Rounds 1-3 (1-3, 1-3): Work in k1, p1 rib.

Fasten off yarn B. Join yarn A with US 9 (5.5mm) straight needles. Work in rows.

Row 4 (4, 4): K2tog, k43 (45, 47), place next 7 (7, 7) stitches on waste yarn, turn. 44 (46, 48) sts.

Row 5-27 (5-29, 5-29): Work in stockinette stitch pattern set.

Row 28 (30, 30): K14 (14, 15), k2tog, k12 (14, 14), k2tog, turn. 42 (44, 46) sts.

Row 29 (31, 31): Sl1 , p12 (14, 14), p2tog, turn. 41 (43, 45) sts.

Row 30 (32, 32): Sl1, k12 (14, 14), k2tog, turn. 40 (42, 44) sts.

Rows 31-50 (33-52, 33-54): Rep. rows last 2 rows, 10 (10, 11) times. 20 (22, 22) sts.

Row 51 (53, 55): Rep. row 29 (31, 31) once. 19 (21, 21) sts.

Row 52 (54, 56): Sl1, [p1, k1]] 5 (6, 6) times, p2tog, k2tog, turn. 17 (19, 19) sts.

Row 53 (55, 57): Sl1, [k1, p1] 5 (6, 6) times, k1, p2tog, turn. 16 (18, 18) sts.

Row 54 (56, 58): Sl1, [p1, k1] 5 (6, 6) times, p1, k2tog, turn. 15 (17, 17) sts.

Row 55 (57, 59): Sl1, [k1, p1] 5 (6, 6) times, k1, p2tog, turn. 14 (16, 16) sts.

NECK RUFF

Work in the round with a US 9 (5.5mm) circular needle.

Round 56 (58, 60): S1, [p1, k1] 5 (6, 6) times, p1, k2tog, pick up and knit 6 (6, 7) stitches along edge, from

waste yarn [p1, k1] 3 (3, 3) times, p1, pick up and knit 6 (6, 7) stitches along edge. 32 (34, 36) sts.

Rounds 57-64 (59-68, 61-72): Work in k1, p1 rib.

Round 65 (69, 73): K1 (2, 2), yo, k2 (2, 2), yo, k7 (7, 7), yo, k2 (2, 2), yo, k5 (6, 7), yo, k2 (2, 2), yo, k7 (7, 7), yo, k2 (2, 2), yo, k4 (4, 5). 40 (42, 44) sts.

Round 66 (70, 74): K2 (3, 3), yo, k2 (2, 2), yo, k9 (9, 9), yo, k2 (2, 2), yo, k7 (8, 9), yo, k2 (2, 2), yo, k9 (9, 9), yo, k2 (2, 2), yo, k5 (5, 6). 48 (50, 52) sts.

Round 67 (71, 75): K3 (4, 4), yo, k2 (2, 2), yo, k11 (11, 11), yo, k2 (2, 2), yo, k9 (10, 11), yo, k2 (2, 2), yo, k11 (11, 11), yo, k2 (2, 2), yo, k6 (6, 7). 56 (58, 60) sts.

Round 68 (72, 76): K4 (5, 5), yo, k2 (2, 2), yo, k13 (13, 13), yo, k2 (2, 2), yo, k11 (12, 13), yo, k2 (2, 2), yo, k13 (13, 13), yo, k2 (2, 2), yo, k7 (7, 8). 64 (66, 68) sts.

Round 69 (73, 77): K5 (6, 6), yo, k2 (2, 2), yo, k15 (15, 15), yo, k2 (2, 2), yo, k13 (14, 15), yo, k2 (2, 2), yo, k15 (15, 15), yo, k2 (2, 2), yo, k8 (8, 9). 72 (74, 76) sts.

Round 70 (74, 78): K6 (7, 7), yo, k2 (2, 2), yo, k17 (17, 17), yo, k2 (2, 2), yo, k15 (16, 17), yo, k2 (2, 2), yo, k17 (17, 17), yo, k2 (2, 2), yo, k9 (9, 10). 80 (82, 84) sts.

2-3 years:

Round 79 : K8, yo, k2, yo, k19, yo, k2, yo, k19, yo, k2, yo, k19, yo, k2, yo, k11. (92) sts.

All sizes:

Fasten off yarn A. Join in yarn B with a US 10 (6mm) circular needle.

Round 71 (75, 80): Knit.

Rounds 72-77 (76-81, 81-86): Work in k1, p1 rib.
Bind off.

EARS
(make 2)

With US 9 (5.5mm) straight needles and A, cast on 20 sts.

Rows 1-5: Work in k1, p1 rib.
Cut yarn, thread through remaining stitches, and draw tight.

Inner ear
(make 2)

With US J-10 (6mm) crochet hook and yarn B: Ch4. Join with sl st to form ring.

Round 1: Ch3, 10dc into the center of ring, join with sl st into top of beg-ch. 11dc.
Finish off.

Finishing

1   Sew inner parts of the ear onto the ears.
2   Sew the ears to the hat in the position shown on page 35.
3   Weave in ends.

MITTENS
(make 2)

With US 10 (6mm) double-pointed needles and A, cast on 16 (18, 18) sts.

CUFF

Rounds 1-6 (1-8, 1-8): Work in K1, p1 rib.

Fasten off yarn B. Join in yarn A. Work using US 9 (5.5mm) double-pointed needles.

Rounds 7-8 (9-10, 9-10): Knit.

THUMB GUSSET

Round 9 (11, 11): K7 (8, 8), m1, k2 (2, 2), m1, k7 (8, 8). 18 (20, 20) sts.

Round 10 (12, 12): Knit.

Round 11 (13, 13): K7 (8, 8), m1, k4 (4, 4), m1, k7 (8, 8). 20 (22, 22) sts.

Round 12 (14, 14): Knit.

Round 13 (15, 15): K7 (8, 8), m1, k6 (6, 6), m1, k7 (8, 8). 22 (24, 24) sts.

Round 14 (16, 16): Knit.

12-24 months and 2-3 years

Round (17, 17): K (8, 8), m1, k (8, 8), m1, k (8, 8). (26, 26) sts.

Round (18, 18): Knit.

All sizes

Round 15 (19, 19): K8 (9, 9), place 6 (8, 8) thumb stitches on waste yarn. Rejoin to work hand stitches in the round, k8 (9, 9). 16 (18, 18) sts.

HAND

Rounds 16-25 (20-30, 20-32): Knit.

Round 26 (31, 33): [K2tog] to end of round. 8 (9, 9) sts.

Round 27 (32, 34): Knit.

Round 28 (33, 35): [K2tog] 4 (4, 4) times, K0 (1, 1). 4 (5, 5) sts. Cut yarn, thread through remaining stitches, and draw tight.

THUMB

Transfer 6 (8, 8) stitches from waste yarn onto needles. Rejoin yarn and pick up and knit 1 st in the corner where mitten meets gusset. 7 (9, 9) sts. Join to work in the round.

Rounds 1-4 (1-5, 1-5): Knit.

Round 5 (6, 6): [K2tog] 3 (4, 4) times, K1 (1, 1). 4 (5, 5) sts. Finish as for mitten Hand.

Finishing

Weave in ends.

This yarn is particularly soft for little hands so it's unlikely a small child will want to yank them off!

zany zebra

This gorgeous zebra is knitted in stripes with pompoms forming a distinctive mane down the back. The fingerless mittens are well designed to keep hands warm but leave the fingers free for playing. Cozy booties complete the set.

Coverall hat, mittens, and booties

LEVEL: intermediate

SIZES
6–12 months (12–24 months, 2–3 years)

Finished measurements
From "cheek to cheek" around the hat: 14½ (15, 15½)in (37 [38, 39]cm)

Mitten circumference: 5 (5½, 5½)in (13 [14, 14]cm)

Mitten length: 5 (5, 6)in (13 [13, 15]cm)

Bootie circumference: 6¼ (6¾, 6¾)in (16 [17, 17]cm)

Bootie length (heel to toe): 4¼ (4, 5)in (11 [12, 13]cm)

Gauge
14 sts and 19 rows = 4in (10cm) square in stockinette stitch worked with US 10 (6mm) needles

15 sts and 19 rows = 4in (10cm) square in k1, p1 rib slightly stretched, worked with US 10 (6mm) needles

Materials

HAT

Yarn:
Color A: 1 x 3.5oz (100g) ball (120yd/109m) Patons Classic Wool Roving Yarn, 100% pure new wool, Black

Color B: 1 x 3.5oz (100g) ball (120yd/109m) Patons Classic Wool Roving Yarn, 100% pure new wool, Aran

Equipment:
- US 10 (6mm) circular needles
- 4 x US 10 (6mm) double-pointed needles
- Optional: Stitch marker to indicate the start of a round
- Yarn needle
- Two circles of cardboard 1¼ in (3cm) in diameter or a pompom maker

FINGERLESS MITTENS

Yarn:
Color A: 1 x 3.5oz (100g) ball (120yd/109m) Patons Classic Wool Roving Yarn, 100% pure new wool, Black

Small amount:
Color B: Patons Classic Wool Roving Yarn, 100% pure new wool, Aran

Equipment:
- 4 x US 10 (6mm) double-pointed needles
- Optional: Stitch marker to indicate the start of a round
- Yarn needle

BOOTIES

Yarn:
Color A: As mittens

Small amounts:
Color B: As mittens

Equipment:
As mittens

Notes:

STRIPE PATTERN REPEAT

Work in stockinette stitch, each stripe starting with a knit row or round.

Rows or rounds 1-2: Yarn B.

Rows or rounds 3-4: Yarn A.

Repeat the last 4 rows or rounds. The photograph shows the stripe pattern as it will appear on the 12-24 month size. The shaping on the smallest size will occur on different rows or rounds of the repeat.

HAT

With US 10 (6mm) circular needle and yarn A, cast on 52 (54, 56) sts. Join to work in the round.

Rounds 1-6 (1-6, 1-6): Work in k1, p1 rib.

Join in yarn B.

Continue to work the hat pattern, while at the same time, working the Stripe pattern repeat, starting with round 1. Do not break yarns, but carry yarns up as you knit.

Row 7 (7, 7): K45 (47, 49), place next 7 (7, 7) stitches on waste yarn, turn. 45 (47, 49) sts.

Row 8 (8, 8): P45 (47, 49), turn.

Rows 9-26 (9-28, 9-28): Work in stockinette stitch pattern set. Work short rows.

Row 27 (29, 29): K14 (15, 15), k2tog, k13 (13, 15), k2tog, turn. 43 (45, 47) sts.

Row 28 (30, 30): Sl1, p13 (13, 15), p2tog, turn. 42 (44, 46) sts.

Row 29 (31, 31): Sl1, k13 (13, 15), k2tog, turn. 41 (43, 45) sts.

Rows 30-53 (32-57, 32-57): Rep. last 2 rows 12 (13, 13) times. 17 (17, 19) sts.

Row 54 (58, 58): Rep. row 28 (30, 30) once. 16 (16, 18) sts.

Follow this photo for the positioning of the pompom mane down the back of the hat.

NECK RUFF

Work in the round with a US 10 (6mm) circular needle.

Round 55 (59, 59): Sl1, k13 (13, 15), k2tog, pick up and knit 10 (10, 10), stitches along edge, from waste yarn k7 (7, 7), pick up and knit 10 (10, 10) stitches along edge. 42 (42, 44) sts.

Rounds 56-62 (60-68, 60-70): Work in stockinette stitch.

Round 63 (69, 71): K1 (1, 2), yo, k2, yo, k9 (9, 9), yo, k2, yo, k8 (8, 9), yo, k2, yo, k9 (9, 9), yo, k2, yo, k7 (7, 7). 50 (50, 52) sts.

Round 64 (70, 72): K2 (2, 3), yo, k2, yo, k11 (11, 11), yo, k2, yo, k10 (10, 11), yo, k2, yo, k11 (11, 11), yo, k2, yo, k8 (8, 8). 58 (58, 60) sts.

Round 65 (71, 73): K3 (3, 4), yo, k2, yo, k13 (13, 13), yo, k2, yo, k12 (12, 13), yo, k2, yo, k13 (13, 13), yo, k2, yo, k9 (9, 9). 66 (66, 68) sts.

Round 66 (72, 74): K4 (4, 5), yo, k2, yo, k15 (15, 15), yo, k2, yo, k14 (14, 15), yo, k2, yo, k15 (15, 15), yo, k2, yo, k10 (10, 10). 74 (74, 76) sts.

Round 67 (73, 75): K5 (5, 6), yo, k2, yo, k17 (17, 17), yo, k2, yo, k16 (16, 17), yo, k2, yo, k17 (17, 17), yo, k2, yo, k11 (11, 11). 82 (82, 84) sts.

Round 68 (74, 76): K6 (6, 7), yo, k2, yo, k19 (19, 19), yo, k2, yo, k18 (18, 19), yo, k2, yo, k19 (19, 19), yo, k2, yo, k12 (12, 12). 90 (90, 92) sts.

12-24 months and 2-3 years:

Round (75, 77): K (7, 8), yo, k2, yo, k (21, 21), yo, k2, yo, k (20, 21), yo, k2, yo, k (21, 21), yo, k2, yo, k (13, 13). (98, 100) sts.

Round (76, 78): K (8, 9), yo, k2, yo, k (23, 23), yo, k2, yo, k (22, 23), yo, k2, yo, k (23, 23), yo, k2, yo, k (14, 14). (106, 108) sts.

2-3 years:

Round 79: K10, *yo, k2, yo, k25* rep. from * to * 3 times, yo, k2, yo, k15. 116 sts.

Round 80: K11, *yo, k2, yo, k27*, rep. from * to * 3 times, yo, k2, yo, k16. 124 sts.

All sizes:

Fasten off yarn B. Continue using yarn A only.

Round 69 (77, 81): Knit.

Rounds 70-75 (78-83, 82-87): Work in k1, p1 rib.

Bind off.

EARS
(make 2)

Using US 10 (6mm) double-pointed needles and yarn A, cast on 8 sts. Join to work in the round.

Rounds 1-2: Knit.

Round 3: [K4, m1] twice. 10 sts.

Round 4: Knit.

Round 5: [K5, m1] twice. 12 sts.

Rounds 6-7: Knit.

Round 8: [K4, k2tog] twice. 10 sts.

Round 9: Knit.

Round 10: [K3, k2tog] twice. 8 sts.

Round 11: Knit.

Round 12: [K2, k2tog] twice. 6 sts.

Round 13: Knit.

Round 14: [K2tog] 3 times. 3 sts.

Cut yarn, thread through remaining stitches, and draw tight.

POMPOMS

Using two circles of cardboard 1¼in (3cm) in diameter or a pompom maker and yarn A, make 5 pompoms.

Finishing

1   Sew the ears to the hat in the position shown on page 39.
2   Sew the pompoms onto the hat.
3   Weave in ends.

Quick and straightforward to make, these fingerless mittens are cleverly designed to keep the whole hand warm.

FINGERLESS MITTENS

(make 2)

With US 10 (6mm) double-pointed needles and yarn A, cast on 16 (18, 18) sts. Join to work in the round.

CUFF

Rounds 1-6 (1-6, 1-6): Work in k1, p1 rib.

Join in yarn B.

Continue to work the Fingerless mitten pattern, while at the same time, working the Hat stripe pattern repeat, starting with row 1. Do not break yarns, but carry yarns up as you knit.

Rounds 7-14 (7-18, 7-18): Knit.

THUMB GUSSET

Round 15 (19, 19): K8 (9, 9), m1, k8 (9, 9). 17 (19, 19) sts.

Round 16 (20, 20): Knit.

Round 17 (21, 21): K8 (9, 9), m1, k1 (1, 1), m1, k8 (9, 9). 19 (21, 21) sts.

Round 18 (22, 22): Knit.

Round 19 (23, 23): K8 (9, 9), m1, k3 (3, 3), m1, k8 (9, 9). 21 (23, 23) sts.

Round 20 (24, 24): Knit.

Fasten off yarn B. Continue using yarn A only.

Round 21 (25, 25): Knit.

Round 22 (26, 26): K8 (9, 9), bind off 5 (5, 5) stitches, k8 (9, 9). 16 (18, 18) sts.

HAND

Rounds 23-25 (27-29, 27-29): Work in k1, p1 rib.

Bind off.

Finishing

Weave in ends.

BOOTIES
(make 2)

With US 10 (6mm) double-pointed needles and yarn A, cast on 22 (24, 24) sts. Join to work in the round.

Rounds 1-6 (1-6, 1-6): Work in k1, p1 rib.

Join in yarn B.

Continue to work the Booties pattern, while at the same time, working the Hat stripe pattern repeat, starting with row 1. Do not break yarns, but carry yarns up as you knit.

Rounds 7-22 (7-26, 7-30): Knit.

HEEL

Work in rows.

Fasten off yarn B. Continue using yarn A only.

Row 23 (27, 31): K11 (12, 12), turn. 11 (12, 12) heel sts.

Row 24 (28, 32): P11 (12, 12), turn.

Rows 25-28 (29-32, 33-36): Rep. rows 23-24 (27-28, 31-32) twice. Work in short rows.

Row 29 (33, 37): K2 (2, 2), k2tog, k3 (4, 4), k2tog, turn.

Row 30 (34, 38): Sl1, p3 (4, 4), p2tog, turn.

Row 31 (35, 39): Sl1, k3, (4, 4), k2tog, turn.

Row 32 (36, 40): Sl1, p3 (4, 4), p2tog, turn. 6 (7, 7) heel sts.

FOOT

Work in rounds.

Round 33 (37, 41): Sl1, k3 (4, 4), k2tog, pick up and knit 3 (3, 3) stitches down side of heel, k11 (12, 12), pick up and knit 3 (3, 3) stitches up side of heel. 22 (24, 24) sts. Work the following partial round to the new starting position for the following rounds.

Round 34 (38, 42): K19 (21, 21). 22 (24, 24) sts.

Place a marker at the beginning of the round.

Round 35 (39, 43): K2tog, k7 (8, 8), k2tog, k11 (12, 12). 20 (22, 22) sts.

Round 36 (40, 44): K2tog, k5 (6, 6), k2tog, k11 (12, 12). 18 (20, 20) sts.

Rounds 37-43 (41-49, 45-55): Knit.

Round 44 (50, 56): [K2tog] rep. to end of round. 9 (10, 10) sts.

Round 45 (51, 57): Knit.

Round 46 (52, 58): [K2tog] 4 (5, 5) times, K1 (0, 0). 5 (5, 5) sts.

Cut yarn, thread through remaining stitches, and draw tight.

Finishing

Weave in ends.

Longer than regular baby booties, these booties are extra warm. They could be worn under rubber boots for outdoor play.

lovely lion

Fun Fur Exotics yarn gives the lion his beautiful fluffy mane and makes this hat extra special. The fur and goggle eyes are repeated on the mittens too. A little simple crocheting is needed to create the eyes.

Materials

Coverall hat and mittens

LEVEL: beginner

SIZES
6-12 months (12-24 months, 2-3 years)

Finished measurements
From "cheek to cheek" around the hat: 16 (16½, 17)in (40.5 [42, 43]cm)
Mitten circumference: 5¾ (6, 6¾)in (14.5 [15, 17]cm)
Mitten length: 5½ (5¾, 7½)in (14 [14.5, 19]cm)

Gauge
16 sts and 24 rows = 4in (10cm) square in stockinette stitch with yarns A and B, worked with US 9 (5.5mm) needles
19 sts and 24 rows = 4in (10cm) square in k1, p1 rib, unstretched, worked with US 9 (5.5mm) needles

HAT

Yarn:
Color A: 1 x 3oz (85g) ball (135yd/123m) Lion Brand Jiffy Yarn, 100% acrylic, Camel
Color B: 2 x 1.75oz (50g) balls (55yd/50m) Lion Brand Fun Fur Exotics Yarn, 100% polyester, Tigers Eye

Small amounts:
Color C: Lion Brand Jiffy Yarn, 100% acrylic, White
Color D: Lion Brand Jiffy Yarn, 100% acrylic, Black
Color E: Lion Brand Jiffy Yarn, 100% acrylic, Gold

Equipment:
- 1 pair of US 9 (5.5mm) needles
- US 9 (5.5mm) circular needles
- US H-8 (5mm) crochet hook
- Optional: Stitch marker to indicate the start of a round
- Yarn needle

MITTENS

Yarn:
Color A: 1 x 3oz (85g) ball (135yd/123m) Lion Brand Jiffy Yarn, 100% acrylic, Camel
Color B: 1 x 1.75oz (50g) ball (55yd/50m) Lion Brand Fun Fur Exotics Yarn, 100% polyester, Tigers Eye

Small amounts:
Color C: Lion Brand Jiffy Yarn, 100% acrylic, White
Color D: Lion Brand Jiffy Yarn, 100% acrylic, Black
Color E: Lion Brand Jiffy Yarn, 100% acrylic, Gold

Equipment:
- 4 x US 9 (5.5mm) double-pointed needles
- Stitch holder
- Optional: Stitch marker to indicate the start of a round
- US H-8 (5mm) crochet hook
- Yarn needle
- Small amount of stuffing (optional)

HAT

With US 9 (5.5mm) straight needles and yarn A, cast on 57 (61, 65) sts.

Rows 1-6 (6, 6): Work in k1, p1 rib. Fasten off yarn A. Join in yarn B.

Rows 7-30 (30, 32): Work in stockinette stitch, starting with a p row.

Work short rows.

Row 31 (31, 33): P18 (20, 21), p2tog, p17 (19, 19), p2tog, turn. 55 (59, 63) sts.

Row 32 (32, 34): Sl1, k17 (19, 19), k2tog, turn. 54 (58, 62) sts.

Row 33 (33, 35): Sl1, p17 (19, 19), p2tog, turn. 53 (57, 61) sts.

Rows 34-53 (34-55, 36-61): Rep. rows last 2 rows 10 (11, 13) times. 33 (35, 35) sts.

Row 54 (56, 62): Rep. row 32 (32, 34) once. 32 (34, 34) sts.

Row 55 (57, 63): Sl1, [k1, p1] 8 (9, 9) times, k1, p2tog, turn. 31 (33, 33) sts.

Row 56 (58, 64): Sl1, [p1, k1] 8 (9, 9) times, p1, k2tog, turn. 30 (32, 32) sts.

Rows 57-66 (59-68, 65-74): Rep. rows last 2 rows 5 (5, 5) times. 20 (22, 22) sts.

NECK RUFF

Work in the round with a US 9 (5.5mm) circular needle.

Round 67 (69, 75): Sl1, [p1, k1] 8 (9, 9) times, p1, k2tog, pick up and knit 13 (12, 12) sts along edge, cast on 7 sts, pick up and knit 13 (12, 12) sts along edge. 52 (52, 52) sts.

Rounds 68-77 (70-81, 76-89): Work in k1, p1 rib.

Round 78 (82, 90): K2 (3, 3), [yo, k2, yo, k11] 3 times, yo, k2, yo, k9 (8, 8). 60 (60, 60) sts.

Round 79 (83, 91): K3 (4, 4), [yo, k2, yo, k13] 3 times, yo, k2, yo, k10 (9, 9). 68 (68, 68) sts.

Round 80 (84, 92): K4 (5, 5), [yo, k2, yo, k15] 3 times, yo, k2, yo, k11 (10, 10). 76 (76, 76) sts.

Rounds 81-83 (85-87, 93-95): Continue in increase pattern set. 100 (100, 100) sts.

12-24 months and 2-3 years:

Rounds (88-89, 96-97): Continue in increase pattern set. (116, 116) sts.

2-3 years:

Rounds 98-99: Continue in increase pattern set. 132 sts.

All sizes:

Rounds 84-89 (90-95, 100-105): Work in k1, p1 rib. Bind off.

EARS

(make 2)

With US 9 (5.5mm) straight needles and yarn A, cast on 20 sts.

Rows 1-4: Work in k1, p1 rib. Cut yarn, thread through remaining stitches, and draw tight.

EYES

(make 2)

With US H-8 (5mm) hook and yarn C: Ch4. Join with sl st to form ring. Work in a spiral. Don't join at the end of a row but continue working.

Round 1: 7sc into the center of ring.

Round 2: 2sc into each sc. 14sc.

Rounds 3-4: 1sc into each sc. 14sc. End with sl st in next st to join. Fasten off.

NOSE

With US 9 (5.5mm) straight needles and yarn D, cast on 5 sts.

Row 1: Knit.

Row 2: K1, m1, k3, m1, k1. 7 sts.

Rows 3-6: Knit.

Row 7: K1, [k2tog, k1] twice. 5 sts.

Row 8: Knit. Fasten off yarn D. Join in yarn E.

Rows 9-18: Knit.

Row 19: K2tog, k1, k2tog. 3 sts.

Row 20: Knit. Bind off.

Finishing

1 Sew the ears to the hat in the position shown on page 45 using an invisible seam.

2 Sew the nose onto the hat.

3 Using yarn D, embroider two small pupils in satin stitch, one for each eye.

4 Tuck the loose yarn ends into the dome of the eyes, and add a tiny bit of stuffing if you want.

5 Sew the eyes onto the hat.

6 Weave in ends.

MITTENS
(make 2)

With US 9 (5.5mm) double-pointed needles and yarn A, cast on 22 (24, 26) sts. Join to work in the round.

Rounds 1-11 (1-13, 1-15): Work in k1, p1 rib.

THUMB GUSSET
Rounds 12-18 (14-21, 16-24): Knit.

Right mitten only:
Round 19 (22, 25): Place first 4 (5, 5) stitches onto waste yarn, cast on 4 (5, 5) stitches (right-hand needle). Rejoin to work in the round, k18 (19, 21). 22 (24, 26) sts.

Left mitten only:
Round 19 (22, 25): K7 (7, 8), place next 4 (5, 5) stitches onto waste yarn, cast on 4 (5, 5) stitches (right-hand needle). Rejoin to work in the round, k11 (12, 13). 22 (24, 26) sts.

Hand
Both mittens:
Rounds 20-21 (23-24, 26-27): Knit.
Fasten off yarn A. Join in yarn B.
Round 22 (25, 28): Knit.
Rounds 23-26 (26-30, 29-33): Purl.
Fasten off yarn B. Join in yarn A.
Rounds 27-32 (31-36, 34-39): Knit.
Round 33 (37, 40): [K2tog] to end of round. 11 (12, 13) sts.
Round 34 (38, 41): Knit.
Round 35 (39, 42): [K2tog] 5 (6, 6) times, K1 (0, 1). 6 (6, 7) sts.
Round 36 (40, 43): Knit.
Cut yarn, thread through remaining stitches, and draw tight.

THUMB
Transfer 4 (5, 5) stitches from waste yarn onto US 9 (5.5mm) double-pointed needles, pick up and knit 4 (5, 5) sts across the 4 (5, 5) cast-on sts. 8 (10, 10) sts. Join to work in the round.
Rounds 1-8 (1-9, 1-10): Knit.
Round 9 (10, 11): [K2tog] to end of round 4 (5, 5) sts.
Finish as for mitten Hand.

EYES
(make 4)

With US H-8 (5mm) crochet hook and C: Ch4. Join with sl st to form ring.
Round 1: 7sc into the center of ring. Join with sl st into top of first st.
Fasten off.

Make sure that you sew the features onto the top of the mitten, taking into account the position of the thumb.

Finishing
1 Using D, embroider two small pupils in satin stitch, one for each eye.
2 Sew the eyes onto the top of the mittens.
3 Using yarn D, embroider the nose in satin stitch, one for each mitten.
4 Weave in ends.

pet loves

cozy cat

This little black cat has sweet knitted pink ears and nose, with crocheted yellow cat eyes. The matching mittens have eye-catching crocheted paws. You could replace the pink yarn in this project with red or another color for a little boy.

Coverall hat and mittens

LEVEL: beginner

SIZES
6-12 months (12-24 months, 2-3 years)

Finished measurements
From "cheek to cheek" around the hat: 14 (14½, 15)in (36 [37, 38]cm)
Mitten circumference: 5½ (6, 6½)in (13.75 [15, 16.25] cm)
Mitten length: 5½ (6½, 7)in (14 [16.5, 18]cm)

Gauge
15 sts and 20 rows = 4in (10cm) square in stockinette stitch worked with US 9 (5.5mm) needles
16 sts and 20 rows = 4in (10cm) square in k1, p1 rib slightly stretched, worked with US 9 (5.5mm) needles

Materials

HAT

Yarn:
Color A: 1 x 3.5oz (100g) ball (148yd/136m) Patons Shetland Chunky Yarn, 75% acrylic, 25% wool, Black

Small amounts:
Color B: Lion Brand, Vanna's Choice Baby Yarn, 100% acrylic, Duckie
Color C: Patons Shetland Chunky Tweeds Yarn, 72% acrylic, 25% wool, 3% viscose, Pretty In Pink

Equipment:
- 1 pair of US 9 (5.5mm) needles
- US 9 (5.5mm) circular needle
- 4 x US 9 (5.5mm) double-pointed needles
- US H-8 (5mm) crochet hook
- Optional: Stitch marker to indicate the start of a round
- Yarn needle

MITTENS

Yarn:
Color A: 1 x 3.5oz (100g) ball (148yd/136m) Patons Shetland Chunky Yarn, 75% acrylic, 25% wool, Black

Small amount:
Color C: Patons Shetland Chunky Tweeds Yarn, 72% acrylic, 25% wool, 3% viscose, Pretty In Pink

Equipment:
- 4 x US 9 (5.5mm) double-pointed needles
- US H-8 (5mm) crochet hook
- Optional: Stitch marker to indicate the start of a round
- Yarn needle

HAT

With US 9 (5.5mm) straight needles, yarn A, cast on 57 (61, 65) sts.

Rows 1-6 (1-6, 1-6): K1, p1 rib.

Rows 7-30 (7-30, 7-32): Work in stockinette st, starting with a k row. Work in short rows.

Row 31 (31, 33): K18 (19, 21), k2tog, k17 (19, 19), k2tog, turn. 55 (59, 63) sts.

Row 32 (32, 34): Sl1, p17 (19, 19), p2tog, turn. 54 (58, 62) sts.

Row 33 (33, 35): Sl1, k17 (19, 19), k2tog, turn. 53 (57, 61) sts.

Rows 34-53 (34-55, 36-61): Rep. last 2 rows 10 (11, 13) times. 33 (35, 35) sts.

Row 54 (56, 62): Rep. row 32 (32, 34) once. 32 (34, 34) sts.

Row 55 (57, 63): Sl1, [p1, k1]] 8 (9, 9) times, p1, k2tog, turn. 31 (33, 33) sts.

Row 56 (58, 64): Sl1, [k1, p1] 8 (9, 9) times, k1, p2tog, turn. 30 (32, 32) sts.

Rows 57-66 (59-68, 65-74): Rep. last 2 rows 5 (5, 5) times. 20 (22, 22) sts.

NECK RUFF

With US 9 (5.5mm) circular needle work in the round.

Round 67 (69, 75): Sl1, [p1, k1] 8 (9, 9) times, p1, k2tog, pick up and knit 13 (12, 12) sts along edge, cast on 7 sts, pick up and knit 13 (12, 12) sts along edge. 52 (52, 52) sts.

Rounds 68-77 (70-81, 76-89): K1, p1 rib.

Round 78 (82, 90): K2 (3, 3), [yo, k2, yo, k11] 3 times, yo, k2, yo, k9 (8, 8). 60 (60, 60) sts.

Round 79 (83, 91): K3 (4, 4), [yo, k2, yo, k13] 3 times, yo, k2, yo, k10 (9, 9). 68 (68, 68) sts.

Round 80 (84, 92): K4 (5, 5), [yo, k2, yo, k15] 3 times, yo, k2, yo, k11 (10, 10). 76 (76, 76) sts.

Round 81-83 (85-87, 93-95): Continue in increase pattern set. 100 (100, 100) sts.

12-24 months:

Rounds 88-97: Continue in increase pattern set. 116 sts

2-3 years:

Rounds 88-99: Continue in increase pattern set. 132 sts.

All sizes:

Rounds 84-89 (90-95, 100-105): K1, p1 rib.

Bind off. Weave in ends.

EARS
(make 2)

With US 9 (5.5mm) double-pointed needles, yarn A, cast on 20 sts. Join to work in the round.

Rounds 1-2: Knit.

Round 3: K2tog, k6, [k2tog] twice, k6, k2tog. 16 sts.

Round 4 and each alt round: Knit.

Round 5: K2tog, k4, [k2tog] twice, k4, k2tog. 12 sts.

Round 7: K2tog, k2, [k2tog] twice, k2, k2tog. 8 sts.

Round 9: [K2tog] 4 times. 4 sts.

Round 10: Knit.

Cut yarn, thread through remaining stitches, and draw tight.

INNER EAR
(make 2)

With US 9 (5.5mm) straight needles, yarn C, cast on 6 sts.

Row 1: Knit.

Row 2 and each alt row: Purl.

Row 3: K2tog, k2, k2tog. 4 sts.

Row 5: [K2tog] twice. 2 sts.

Cut yarn, thread through remaining stitches, and draw tight.

EYES
(make 2)

With US H-8 (5mm) hook and yarn B: Ch4.

Round 1: Into the first ch, work [6dc, 1dtr, 6dc], sl st into the top of the beg-ch, into the same ch, work [1dc, ch1, 1sc, ch1, 1dc, ch2, sl st]. Fasten off.

Finishing

1 Sew Inner ears onto the Ears.

2 Using the photograph on page 51 as a guide, sew the Ears and Eyes onto the hat.

3 Using yarn A embroider small pupils on eyes in satin stitch.

4 Weave in ends.

MITTENS
(make 2)

With US 9 (5.5mm) double-pointed needles, yarn A, cast on 22 (24, 26) sts. Join to work in the round.

CUFF
Rounds 1-10 (1-12, 1-14): Work in k1, p1 rib.

THUMB GUSSET
Round 11 (13, 15): M1, knit to end of round. 23 (25, 27) sts.
Round 12 (14, 16) and each alt round: Knit.
Round 13 (15, 17): M1, k3, m1, k20 (22, 24). 25 (27, 29) sts.
Round 15 (17, 19): M1, k5, m1, k20 (22, 24). 27 (29, 31) sts.
Round 17 (19, 21): M1, k7, m1, k20 (22, 24). 29 (31, 33) sts.
Round 18 (20, 22): Knit.

12-24 months and 2-3 years:
Round (21, 23): M1, k9, m1, k (22, 24). (33, 35) sts.

All sizes:
Round 19 (22, 24): K1, place 7 (9, 9) on waste yarn. Rejoin to work hand stitches in the round, k21 (23, 25). 22 (24, 26) sts.

HAND
Rounds 20-32 (23-38, 25-42): Knit.
Round 33 (39, 43): [K2tog] to end of round. 11 (12, 13) sts.
Round 34 (40, 44): Knit.
Round 35 (41, 45): [K2tog] 5 (6, 6) times, K1 (0, 1). 6 (6, 7) sts.
Cut yarn, thread through remaining stitches, and draw tight.

THUMB
Transfer 7 (9, 9) sts from waste yarn onto needles. Rejoin yarn A, pick up and knit 1 st. 8 (10, 10) sts. Join to work in the round.
Rounds 1-6 (1-6, 1-8): Knit.
Round 7 (7, 9): [K2tog] to end of round. 4 (5, 5) sts.
Finish as for mitten Hand.

PAWS
Small circles (make 6)
With US H-8 (5mm) hook, yarn C: Ch4. Join with sl st to form ring.
Round 1: 7sc into the ring. Join with sl st to the first st.
Fasten off.

Large circles (make 2)
With US H-8 (5mm) hook, yarn C: Ch4. Join with sl st to form ring.
Round 1: Ch2, 13dc into the ring. 14dc. Join with sl st to top of beg ch. Fasten off.

Finishing
1 Sew the paws onto the mitten as shown below.
2 Weave in ends.

As for the hat, you could use a different color to create the crocheted-circle paws for a little boy.

floppy bunny

If you're looking for a no-nonsense coverall hat in a plain color, the floppy bunny is perfect. The long ears can flop forward or backward, creating the rabbit character without the need for additional features.

Materials

Coverall hat and mittens

LEVEL: intermediate

SIZES
6-12 months (12-24 months, 2-3 years)

Finished measurements
From "cheek to cheek" around the hat: 15 (15½, 16)in (38 [39.5, 40.5]cm)
Mitten circumference: 5½ (6, 6½)in (13.75 [15, 16.25]cm)
Mitten length: 5½ (6½, 7)in (14 [16.5, 18]cm)

Gauge
17 sts and 24 rows = 4in (10cm) square in stockinette stitch worked with US 8 (5mm) needles
19 sts and 24 rows = 4in (10cm) square in k1, p1 rib unstretched, worked with US 8 (5mm) needles.

HAT

Yarn:
1 x 3oz (85g) ball (135yd/123m) Lion Brand Jiffy Yarn, 100% acrylic, Taupe Mist

Equipment:
- US 8 (5mm) circular needle
- 4 x US 8 (5mm) double-pointed needles
- 2 x Stitch holders
- Optional: Stitch marker to indicate the start of a round
- Yarn needle

MITTENS

Yarn:
1 x 3oz (85g) ball (135yd/123m) Lion Brand Jiffy Yarn, 100% acrylic, Taupe Mist

Equipment:
- 4 x US 8 (5mm) double-pointed needles
- Optional: Stitch marker to indicate the start of a round
- Yarn needle

HAT

With a US 8 (5mm) circular needle, cast on 63 (66, 69) sts.
Join to work in the round.
Rounds 1-5 (1-7, 1-7): Work in k2, p1 rib.
Work in rows.
Row 6 (8, 8): P55 (58, 61), place next 8 (8, 8) stitches onto waste yarn, turn. 55 (58, 61) sts.
Row 7 (9, 9): K55 (58, 61), turn.
Rows 8-30 (10-34, 10-36): Knit.
Work short rows.
Row 31 (35, 37): K17 (18, 19), k2tog, k3 (4, 4), place next 4 (4, 4) stitches onto stitch holder, cast on 4 (4, 4) stitches, k3 (2, 3), place next 4 (4, 4) stitches onto stitch holder, cast on 4 (4, 4) stitches, k3 (4, 4), k2tog, turn. 53 (56, 59) sts.
Row 32 (36, 38): Sl1, p17 (18, 19), p2tog, turn. 52 (55, 58) sts.
Row 33 (37, 39): Sl1, k17 (18, 19), k2tog, turn. 51 (54, 57) sts.
Rows 34-55 (38-59, 40-61): Rep. last 2 rows, 11 times. 29 (32, 35) sts.

6-12 months:
Row 56: Sl1, p1, k2tog, [p2, k1] 3 times, p2, k2tog, p1, p2tog, turn. 26 sts.
Row 57: Sl1, k1, [p1, k2] 4 times, p1, k1, k2tog, turn. 25 sts.
Row 58: Sl1, p1, [k1, p2] 4 times, k1, p1, p2tog, turn. 24 sts.
Rows 59-64: Rep. last 2 rows, 3 times. 18 sts.

12-24 months:
Row 60: Sl1, p1, [k1, p2] 5 times, k1, p1, p2tog, turn, (20 sts worked). 31 sts.
Row 61: Sl1, k1, [p1, k2] 5 times, p1, k1, k2tog, turn, (20 sts worked). 30 sts.
Rows 62-69 : Rep. last 2 rows, 4 times. 22 sts.
Row 70: Rep. row 60 once. 21 sts.

2-3 years:
Row 62: Sl1, p1, [k1, p2] 5 times, k2tog, p1, p2tog, turn. 33 sts.
Row 63: Sl1, k1, [p1, k2] 5 times, p1, k1, k2tog, turn. 32 sts.
Row 64: Sl1, p1, [k1, p2] 5 times, k1, p1, p2tog, turn. 31 sts.
Rows 65-74: Rep. last 2 rows, 5 times. 21 sts.

NECK RUFF
All sizes
Work in the round.
Round 65 (71, 75): Sl1, k1, [p1, k2] 4 (5, 5) times, p1, k1, k2tog, pick up and knit 13 (13, 13) stitches along edge, from waste yarn k2, p1, k2, p1, k2 , pick up and knit 13 (13, 13) stitches along edge. 51 (54, 54) sts.
Rounds 66-76 (72-82, 76-88): K2, p1 rib.

6-12 months:
Round 77: K2, m1, k6, m1, k5, m1, *k6, m1, k6, m1, k5, m1* rep. from * to * twice, k4. 60 sts.
Round 78: Knit.
Round 79: K2, m1, k7, m1, k6, m1, *k7, m1, k7, m1, k6, m1* rep. from * to * twice, k5. 69 sts.
Round 80: Knit.
Round 81: K2, m1, k8, m1, k7, m1, *k8, m1, k8, m1, k7, m1* rep. from * to * twice, k6. 78 sts.

Round 82: Knit.
Round 83-86: Continue in increase pattern set. 96 sts.

12-24 months and 2-3 years:
Round (83, 89): K2, m1, *k6, m1* rep. from * to * 8 times, k4. (63, 63) sts.
Round (84, 90): Knit.
Round (85, 91): K2, m1, *k7, m1* rep. from * to * 8 times, k5. (72, 72) sts.
Round (86, 92): Knit.
Round (87, 93): K2, m1, *k8, m1* rep. from * to * 8 times, k6. (81, 81) sts.
Round (88, 94): Knit.
Round (89-92, 95-98): Continue in increase pattern set. (99, 99) sts.

2-3 years:
Round 99-100: Continue in increase pattern set. (108) sts.

All sizes:
Rounds 87-93 (93-99, 101-107): K2, p1 rib.
Bind off.

EARS
(make 2)
Transfer 4 stitches from stitch holder onto US 8 (5mm) double-pointed needles, pick up one extra stitch, pick up 4 stitches from 4 cast-on stitches, pick up one extra stitch. 10 sts. Join to work in the round.
Rounds 1-2: Knit.
Round 3: K1, m1, k2, m1, k3, m1, k2, m1, k2. 14 sts.
Rounds 4-9: Knit.
Round 10: [K7, m1] twice. 16 sts.

Rounds 11-16: Knit.
Round 17: [K8, m1] twice. 18 sts.
Rounds 18-23: Knit.
Round 24: [K9, m1] twice. 20 sts.
Rounds 25-30: Knit.
Round 31: [K8, k2tog] twice. 18 sts.
Rounds 32-37: Knit.
Round 38: [K7, k2tog] twice. 16 sts.
Rounds 39-44: Knit.
Round 45-62: Continue in decrease pattern set.
Round 63: [K2, k2tog] twice. 6 sts.
Round 64: Knit.
Round 65: [K1, k2tog] twice. 4 sts.
Round 66: [K2tog] twice. 2 sts.
Cut yarn, thread through remaining stitches, and draw tight

Finishing
1   Sew the ears onto the hat.
2   Weave in ends..

These simple mittens have long cuffs to prevent them slipping off and to keep little hands snug.

MITTENS
(make 2)
With US 8 (5mm) double-pointed needles, cast on 24 (27, 27) sts. Join to work in the round.
Rounds 1-16 (1-18, 1-20): Work in K2, p1 rib.

THUMB GUSSET
Round 17 (19, 21): K4 (4, 4), m1, k16 (19, 19), m1, k4 (4, 4). 26 (29, 29) sts.
Round 18 (20, 22) and each alt round: Knit.
Round 19 (21, 23): K4 (4, 4), m1, k18 (21, 21), m1, k4 (4, 4). 28 (31, 31) sts.
Round 21 (23, 25): K4 (4, 4), m1, k20 (23, 23), m1, k4 (4, 4). 30 (33, 33) sts.

2-3 years:
Round 27: K4, m1, k25, m1, k4. 35 sts.

All sizes
Round 22 (24, 28): K26 (29, 31), place next 4 stitches and first 4 stitches from next round onto waste yarn. 22 (25, 27) sts.
Rounds 23-35 (25-39, 29-45): Knit.
Round 37 (40, 46): [K2tog] 11 (12, 13) times, K0 (1, 1). 11 (13, 14) sts.
Round 38 (41, 47): Knit.
Round 39 (42, 48): [K2tog] 5 (6, 7) times, K1 (1, 0). 6 (7, 7) sts.
Cut yarn, thread through remaining stitches, and draw tight.

THUMB
Transfer 8 (8, 8) stitches from waste yarn onto needles. Rejoin yarn and pick up one extra stitch in the corner where mitten meets the gusset. 9 (9, 9) sts.
Rounds 1-6 (1-7, 1-8): Knit.
Round 7 (8, 9): [K2tog] 4 (4, 4) times, K1 (1, 1). 5 (5, 5) sts.
Finish as for mitten Hand.

Finishing
Weave in ends.

darling dog

The long, floppy ears knitted on double-pointed needles, and the small round crochet nose and embroidered eyes, give this precious pup his personality. Simple striped mittens match the coverall hat.

Materials

Coverall hat and mittens

LEVEL: beginner

SIZES
6-12 months (12-24 months, 2-3 years)

Finished measurements
From "cheek to cheek" around the hat: 14½ (15, 15½)in (37 [38, 39]cm)
Mitten circumference: 5½ (6, 6)in (14 [15, 15]cm)
Mitten length: 5½ (6½, 7½)in (14 [16.5, 19]cm)

Gauge
14 sts and 19 rows = 4in (10cm) square in stockinette stitch worked with US 10 (6mm) needles
15 sts and 19 rows = 4in (10cm) square in k1, p1 rib slightly stretched, worked with US 10 (6.mm) needles

HAT

Yarn:
Color A: 1 x 3.5oz (100g) ball (120yd/109m) Patons Classic Wool Roving Yarn, 100% pure new wool, Pumpkin

Small amounts:
Color B: Patons Classic Wool Roving Yarn, 100% pure new wool, Aran
Color C: Patons Classic Wool Roving Yarn, 100% pure new wool, Yellow
Color D: Patons Classic Wool Roving Yarn, 100% pure new wool, Taupe

Equipment:
• US 10 (6mm) circular needle
• US H-8 (5mm) crochet hook
• Optional: Stitch marker to indicate the start of a round
• Yarn needle

MITTENS

Yarn:
Color A: 1 x 3.5oz (100g) ball (120yd/109m) Patons Classic Wool Roving Yarn, 100% pure new wool, Pumpkin

Small amounts:
Color B: Patons Classic Wool Roving Yarn, 100% pure new wool, Aran
Color C: Patons Classic Wool Roving Yarn, 100% pure new wool, Yellow

Equipment:
• 4 x US 10 (6mm) double-pointed needles
• Optional: Stitch marker to indicate the start of a round
• Yarn needle

HAT

With a US 10 (6mm) circular needle and yarn B, cast on 52 (54, 56) sts. Join to work in the round.

Rounds 1-2 (1-2, 1-2): Work in k1, p1 rib.

Fasten off yarn B. Join in yarn C.

Round 3 (3, 3): Knit.

Round 4 (4, 4): Work in K1, p1 rib.

Fasten off yarn C. Join in yarn A.

Round 5 (5, 5): Knit.

Round 6 (6, 6): Work in K1, p1 rib. Work in rows.

Row 7 (7, 7): K45 (47, 49), place next 7 (7, 7) stitches on waste yarn, turn. 45 (47, 49) sts.

Row 8 (8, 8): P45 (47, 49), turn.

Rows 9-26 (9-28, 9-28): Work in stockinette stitch pattern set. Work short rows.

Row 27 (29, 29): K14 (15, 15), k2tog, k13 (13, 15), k2tog, turn. 43 (45, 47) sts.

Row 28 (30, 30): Sl1, p13 (13, 15), p2tog, turn. 42 (44, 46) sts.

Row 29 (31, 31): Sl1, k13 (13, 15), k2tog, turn. 41 (43, 45) sts.

Rows 30-53 (32-57, 32-57): Rep. last 2 rows 12 (13, 13) times. 17 (17, 19) sts.

Row 54 (58, 58): Rep. row 28 (30, 30) once. 16 (16, 18) sts.

NECK RUFF

Work in the round.

Round 55 (59, 59): Sl1, k13 (13, 15), k2tog, pick up and knit 10 (10, 10), along edge, k7 (7, 7) stitches from waste yarn, pick up and knit 10 (10, 10) stitches along edge. 42 (42, 44) sts.

This back view of the hat shows off its neat fitting around the head and shoulders.

Use the photos as a guide for ear, eye, and nose placement.

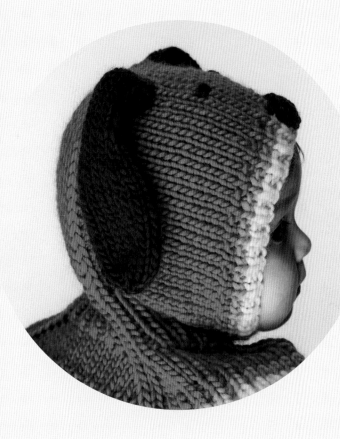

Rounds 56-62 (60-68, 60-70): Work in k1, p1 rib.

Round 63 (69, 71): K1 (1, 2), yo, k2, yo, k9 (9, 9), yo, k2, yo, k8 (8, 9), yo, k2, yo, k9 (9, 9), yo, k2, yo, k7 (7, 7). 50 (50, 52) sts.

Round 64 (70, 72): K2 (2, 3), yo, k2, yo, k11 (11, 11), yo, k2, yo, k10 (10, 11), yo, k2, yo, k11 (11, 11), yo, k2, yo, k8 (8, 8). 58 (58, 60) sts.

Round 65 (71, 73): K3 (3, 4), yo, k2, yo, k13 (13, 13), yo, k2, yo, k12 (12, 13), yo, k2, yo, k13 (13, 13), yo, k2, yo, k9 (9, 9). 66 (66, 68) sts.

Round 66-68 (72-74, 74-76): Work in increase pattern set. (90, 92) sts.

12-24 months and 2-3 years:

Round (75, 77): Work in increase pattern set. (98, 100) sts.

2-3 years:

Round 78: Work in increase pattern set. (108) sts.

All sizes:

Rounds 69-70 (76-77, 79-80): Work in k1, p1 rib.
Fasten off yarn A. Join in yarn C.

Round 71 (78, 81): Knit.

Round 72 (79, 82): Work in k1, p1 rib.
Fasten off yarn C. Join in yarn B.

The way many of these coverall hats are constructed will allow two panels of stockinette stitch to meet at an angle, creating a seam and these lovely patterns.

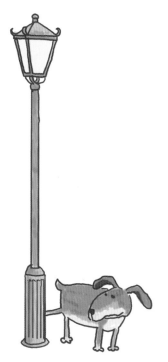

Round 73 (80, 83): Knit.
Rounds 74-75 (81-82, 84-85):
Work in k1, p1 rib.
Bind off.

EARS
(make 2)
With US 10 (6mm) double-pointed needles and yarn D, cast on 8 sts. Join to work in the round.
Rounds 1-7: Knit.
Round 8: K4, m1, k4. 9 sts.
Rounds 9-10: Knit.
Round 11: K4, m1, k1, m1, k4. 11 sts.
Rounds 12-13: Knit.
Round 14: K4, m1, k3, m1, k4. 13 sts.
Rounds 15-17: Knit.
Round 18: K4, m1, k5, m1, k4. 15 sts.
Rounds 19-21: Knit.
Round 22: K4, m1, k7, m1, k4. 17 sts.
Rounds 23-32: Knit.

Round 33: [K2tog] 8 times, k1. 9 sts.
Round 34: [K2tog] 4 times, k1. 5 sts.
Cut yarn, thread through remaining stitches, and draw tight.

NOSE
With US H-8 (5mm) crochet hook and yarn D: Ch3. Join with sl st to form ring.
Round 1: Ch2, work into the center of ring [3hdc, 3dc, 3hdc, 3dc]. Join with sl st on top beg-ch. Fasten off.

Finishing
1 Sew the ears onto the hat.
2 Sew the nose onto the hat.
3 Embroider two eyes in satin stitch.
4 Weave in ends.

MITTENS
(make 2)

With US 10 (6mm) double-pointed needles and yarn A, cast on 16 (18, 18) sts. Join to work in the round.

CUFF
Rounds 1-6 (1- 8, 1-8): Work in k1, p1 rib.
Rounds 7-8 (9-10, 9-10): Knit.

THUMB GUSSET
Round 9 (11, 11): K7 (8, 8), m1, k2 (2, 2), m1, k7 (8, 8). 18 (20, 20) sts.
Round 10 (12, 12) and each alt round: Knit.
Round 11 (13, 13): K7 (8, 8), m1, k4 (4, 4), m1, k7 (8, 8). 20 (22, 22) sts.
Round 13 (15, 15): K7 (8, 8), m1, k6 (6, 6), m1, k7 (8, 8). 22 (24, 24) sts.
Round 14 (16, 16): Knit.

12-24 months and 2-3years
Round (17, 17): K(8, 8), m1, k(8, 8), m1, k(8, 8). (26, 26) sts.
Round (18, 18): Knit.

All sizes
Round 15 (19, 19): K8 (9, 9), place 6 (8, 8) thumb stitches on waste yarn. Rejoin to work hand stitches in the round, k8 (9, 9). 16 (18, 18) sts.

HAND
Rounds 16-19 (20-24, 20-26): Knit.
Fasten off yarn A. Join in yarn C.
Rounds 20-21 (25-26, 27-28): Knit.
Fasten off yarn C. Join in yarn B.
Rounds 22-25 (27-30, 29-32): Knit.
Round 26 (31, 33): [K2tog] to end of round. 8 (9, 9) sts.
Round 27 (32, 34): Knit.
Round 28 (33, 35): [K2tog] 4 (4, 4) times, K0 (1, 1). 4 (5, 5) sts.
Cut yarn, thread through remaining stitches, and draw tight.

THUMB
Transfer 6 (8, 8) stitches from waste yarn in yarn A onto needles. Rejoin yarn and pick up one extra stitch in the corner where mitten meets gusset. 7 (9, 9) sts.
Join to work in the round.
Rounds 1-4 (1-5, 1-5): Knit.
Round 5 (6, 6): [K2tog] 3 (4, 4) times, K1 (1, 1). 4 (5, 5) sts.
Finish as for mitten Hand.

Finishing
Weave in ends.

The stripes mirror the colors on the front of the hat but you could substitute dark brown for one of the colors if you prefer.

mini mouse

This unusual hat is knitted in garter stitch and has an attractive heart-shaped opening for the face and scalloped inner ears. The neck ruff is secured at the front with buttons. There is no crocheting in this project.

Coverall hat and mittens

LEVEL: intermediate

SIZES
6–12 months (12–24 months, 2–3 years)

Finished measurements
From "cheek to cheek" around the hat: 14½ (15, 15½)in (37 [38, 39]cm)

Mitten circumference: 5½ (6, 6½)in (13.75 [15, 16.25]cm)

Mitten length: 5½ (6, 6½)in (14 [15.5, 16.5]cm)

Gauge
20 sts and 36 rows = 4in (10cm) square in garter stitch worked with US 8 (5mm) needles

Materials

HAT

Yarn:
Color A: 1 x 3oz (85g) ball (135yd/123m) Lion Brand Jiffy Yarn, 100% acrylic, Silver Heather

Small amount:
Color B: Lion Brand Jiffy Yarn, 100% acrylic, Light Pink

Equipment:
- 1 pair of US 8 (5mm) needles
- Optional: Stitch marker to indicate the start of a round
- Yarn needle
- 3 buttons

MITTENS

Yarn:
Color A: 1 x 3oz (85g) ball (135yd/123m) Lion Brand Jiffy Yarn, 100% acrylic, Silver Heather

Equipment:
- 4 x US 8 (5mm) double-pointed needles
- Optional: Stitch marker to indicate the start of a round
- Yarn needle

HAT

With US 8 (5mm) straight needles, cast on 60 (62, 64) sts.
Work in garter stitch.
Row 1 (1, 1): Knit.
Row 2 (2, 2): K20 (21, 22), m1, k8 (8, 8), [k2tog] twice, k8 (8, 8), m1, k20 (21, 22). 60 (62, 64) sts.
Rows 3-16 (3-16, 3-16): Rep. last 2 rows 7 (7, 7) times. 60 (62, 64) sts.
Rows 17-39 (17-41, 17-41): Knit.
Work short rows.
Row 40 (42, 42): K19 (20, 21), k2tog, k18 (18, 18), k2tog, turn. 58 (60, 62) sts.
Row 41 (43, 43): K19 (19, 19), k2tog, turn. 57 (59, 61) sts.
Rows 42-65 (44-69, 44-71): Rep. last 2 rows 24 (26, 28) times. 33 (33, 33) sts.
Row 66 (70, 72): K3 (3, 3), k2tog, k10 (10, 10), k2tog, k2 (2, 2), k2tog, turn. 30 (30, 30) sts.
Row 67 (71, 73): K17 (17, 17), k2tog, turn. 29 (29, 29) sts.
Rows 68-69 (72-73, 74-75): Rep. row 67 (71, 73), twice. 27 (27, 27) sts.
Row 70 (74, 76): K3 (3, 3), k2tog, k8 (8, 8), k2tog, k2 (2, 2), k2tog, turn. 24 (24, 24) sts.
Row 71 (75, 77): K15 (15, 15), k2tog, turn. 23 (23, 23) sts.
Rows 72-76 (76-80, 78-82): Rep. row 71 (75, 77) 5 times. 18 (18, 18) sts.
Row 77 (81, 83): K3 (3, 3), k2tog, k6 (6, 6), k2tog, k2 (2, 2), k2tog, turn. 15 (15, 15) sts.

NECK RUFF

Row 78 (82, 84): K13 (13, 13), k2tog, pick up and knit along edge 18 (19, 20) stitches, cast on 8 (8, 8) sts, turn. 40 (41, 42) sts.
Row 79 (83, 85): K40 (41, 42), pick up and purl 18 (19, 20) stitches, along edge, cast on 8 (8, 8) sts, turn. 66 (68, 70) sts.
Rows 80-82 (84-86, 86-88): Knit.
Row 83 (87, 89): K4 (4, 4), yo, k2tog, k60 (62, 64). 66 (68, 70) sts.
Rows 84-92 (88-98, 90-100): Knit.
Row 93 (99, 101): Rep. row 83 (87, 89).
Rows 94-100 (100-106, 102-108): Knit.

6-12 months:

Row 101: K5, m1, [k7, m1] 8 times, k5. 75 sts.
Rows 102: Knit.
Row 103: K4, yo, k2tog, k1, [m1, k8] 8 times, m1, k4. 84 sts.

12-24 months:

Row 107: K6, m1, [k7, m1] 8 times, k6. 77 sts.
Rows 108-110: Knit.
Row 111: K4, yo, k2tog, k1, [m1, k8] 8 times, m1, k6. 86 sts.

2-3 years:

Row 109: [K7, m1] 9 times, k7. 79 sts.
Rows 110-112: Knit.
Row 113: K4, yo, k2tog, k1, [m1, k8] 9 times. 88 sts.

All sizes:

Rows 104-106 (112-114, 114-116): Knit.
Row 107 (115, 117): K6 (7, 8), m1, [k9 (9, 9), m1] 8 (8, 8) times, k6 (7, 8). 93 (95, 97) sts.
Rows 108-110 (116-118, 118-120): Knit.
Bind off.

EARS
(make 2)

With US 8 (5mm) straight needles and yarn A, cast on 30 sts.
Rows 1-5: Knit.
Row 6: [K2, k2tog] 7 times, k2. 23 sts.
Rows 7-10: Work in k1, p1 rib.
Cut yarn, thread through remaining stitches, and draw tight.

INNER EAR
(make 2)

With US 8 (5mm) straight needles and yarn B, cast on 19 sts.
Rounds 1-5: Work in 1, p1 rib.
Cut yarn, thread through remaining stitches, and draw tight.

Finishing

1 Sew inner parts of the ear onto the ears.
2 Sew the ears to the hat in the position shown on page 65.
3 Sew the buttons onto the hat.
4 Weave in ends.

MITTENS
(make 2)

With US 8 (5mm) double-pointed needles and yarn A, cast on 18 (20, 22) sts. Join to work in the round.

CUFF

Round 1 (1, 1): Knit.
Round 2 (2, 2): Purl.
Rounds 3-14 (3-16, 3-18): Rep. last 2 rounds, 6 (7, 8) times.

6-12 months only:

Round 15 : [K6, m1] 3 times. 21 sts.

12-24 months and 2-3 years:

Round (17, 19): [K (7, 7), m1] twice, k (6, 8), m1. (23, 25) sts.
Round 16 (18, 20): Purl.
Round 17 (19, 21): Knit.
Round 18 (20, 22): Purl.

THUMB GUSSET

Round 19 (21, 23): K9 (10, 11), m1, k3 (3, 3), m1, k9 (10, 11). 23 (25, 27) sts.
Round 20 (22, 24): Purl.
Round 21 (23, 25): K9 (10, 11), m1, k5 (5, 5), m1, k9 (10, 11). 25 (27, 29) sts.
Round 22 (24, 26): Purl.
Round 23 (25, 27): K9 (10, 11), m1, k7 (7, 7), m1, k9 (10, 11). 27 (29, 31) sts.
Round 24 (26, 28): Purl.
Round 25 (27, 29): K10 (11, 12), place 7 (7, 7) thumb stitches on waste yarn. Rejoin to work hand stitches in the round, k10 (11, 12). 20 (22, 24) sts.

HAND

Round 26 (28, 30): Purl.
Round 27 (29, 31): Knit.

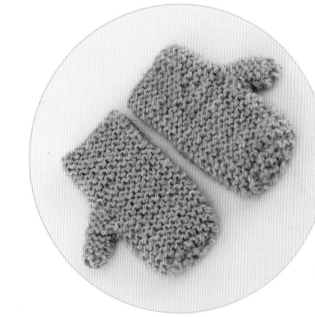

The mittens are knitted in the same pattern as the hat; unusually, they do not have ribbed cuffs, giving a lighter, looser fit.

Rounds 28-39 (30-43, 32-47): Rep. last 2 rounds 6 (7, 8) times. 20 (22, 24) sts.
Round 40 (44, 48): Purl.
Round 41 (45, 49): [K2tog] to end of round. 10 (11, 12) sts.
Round 42 (46, 50): Purl.
Round 43 (47, 51): [K2tog] 5 (5, 6) times, K0 (1, 0). 5 (6, 6) sts.
Cut yarn, thread through remaining stitches, and draw tight.

THUMB

Transfer 7 (7, 7) stitches from waste yarn onto needles. Rejoin yarn and pick up one extra stitch in the corner where mitten meets gusset. 8 (8, 8) sts.

Join to work in the round.
Round 1 (1, 1): Knit.
Round 2 (2, 2): Purl.
Rounds 3-8 (3-8, 3-10): Rep. last 2 rounds, 3 (3, 4) times.
Round 9 (9, 11): [K2tog] to end of round. 4 (4, 4) sts.
Finish as for mitten Hand.

Finishing

Weave in ends.

bear hugs

beauty bear

Little girls will love this hat with its crocheted flower complete with tiny leaves. Why not make it without the flower for a little boy? The matching cream and gray mittens are suitable for both boys and girls.

Coverall hat and mittens

LEVEL: beginner

SIZES
6-12 months (12-24 months, 2-3 years)

Finished measurements
From "cheek to cheek" around the hat: 14½ (15, 15½)in (37 [38, 39]cm)
Mitten circumference: 5½ (6, 6½)in (13.75 [15, 16.25]cm)
Mitten length: 5½ (6½, 7)in (14 [16.5, 18]cm)

Gauge
15 sts and 20 rows = 4in (10cm) square in stockinette stitch worked with US 9 (5.5mm) needles
16 sts and 20 rows = 4in (10cm) square in k1, p1 rib unstretched worked with US 9 (5.5mm) needles

Materials

HAT

Yarn:
Color A: 1 x 3.5oz (100g) ball (148yd/136m) Patons Shetland Chunky Yarn, 75% acrylic, 25% wool, Aran

Small amount:
Color B: Patons Shetland Chunky Yarn, 72% acrylic, 25% wool, 3% viscose, Pewter

Equipment:
- 1 pair of US 9 (5.5mm) needles
- US 9 (5.5mm) circular needle
- US H-8 (5mm) crochet hook
- Optional: Stitch marker to indicate the start of a round
- Yarn needle

MITTENS

Yarn:
Color A: 1 x 3.5oz (100g) ball (148yd/136m) Patons Shetland Chunky Yarn, 75% acrylic, 25% wool, Aran

Small amount:
Color B: Patons Shetland Chunky Tweeds Yarn, 72% acrylic, 25% wool, 3% viscose, Pewter

Equipment:
- 4 x US 9 (5.5mm) double-pointed needles
- Optional: Stitch marker to indicate the start of a round
- Yarn needle

HAT

With US 9 (5.5mm) straight needles and yarn B, cast on 57 (61, 65) sts.

Rows 1-6 (1-6, 1-6): Work in k1, p1, rib.

Fasten off yarn B. Join in yarn A.

Rows 7-30 (7-30, 7-32): Work in stockinette stitch, starting with a k row.

Work short rows.

Row 31 (31, 33): K18 (19, 21), k2tog, k17 (19, 19), k2tog, turn. 55 (59, 63) sts.

Row 32 (32, 34): Sl1, p17 (19, 19), p2tog, turn. 54 (58, 62) sts.

Row 33 (33, 35): Sl1, k17 (19, 19), k2tog, turn. 53 (57, 61) sts.

Rows 34-53 (34-55, 36-61): Rep. last 2 rows 10 (11, 13) times. 33 (35, 35) sts.

Row 54 (56, 62): Rep. row 32 (32, 34) once. 32 (34, 34) sts.

Row 55 (57, 63): Sl1, [p1, k1] 8 (9, 9) times, p1, k2tog, turn. 31 (33, 33) sts.

Row 56 (58, 64): Sl1, [k1, p1] 8 (9, 9) times, k1, p2tog, turn. 30 (32, 32) sts.

Rows 57-66 (59-68, 65-74): Rep. the last 2 rows 5 (5, 5) times. 20 (22, 22) sts.

NECK RUFF

With a US 9 (5.5mm) circular needle, work in the round.

Round 67 (69, 75): Sl1, [p1, k1] 8 (9, 9) times, p1, k2tog, pick up and knit 13 (12, 12) sts along edge, cast on 7 sts, pick up and knit 13 (12, 12) sts along edge. 52 (52, 52) sts.

Use the photos to establish the correct placement of the ears and the flower.

For an extra splash of color, replace yarn B with a colorful variation of your choice.

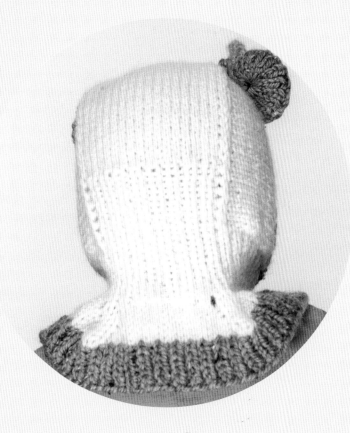

Rounds 68-77 (70-81, 76-89): Work in k1, p1, rib.
Round 78 (82, 90): K2 (3, 3), [yo, k2, yo, k11] 3 times, yo, k2, yo, k9 (8, 8). 60 (60, 60) sts.
Round 79 (83, 91): K3 (4, 4), [yo, k2, yo, k13] 3 times, yo, k2, yo, k10 (9, 9). 68 (68, 68) sts.
Round 80 (84, 92): K4 (5, 5), [yo, k2, yo, k15 (15, 15)] 3 times, yo, k2, yo, k11 (10, 10). 76 (76, 76) sts.
Round 81-83 (85-87, 93-95): Continue in increase pattern set. 100 (100, 100) sts.

12-24 months and 2-3 years:
Round (88-89, 96-97): Continue in increase pattern set. (116, 116) sts.

2-3 years only:
Round 98-99: Continue in increase pattern set. 132 sts.

All sizes:
Rounds 84-89 (90-95, 100-105): Work in k1, p1, rib.
Bind off.

EARS
(make 2)
With US 9 (5.5mm) straight needles and yarn B, cast on 25 sts.
Rows 1-5: Work in k1, p1, rib.
Cut yarn, thread through remaining stitches, and draw tight.

Repeat the flower pattern as many times as you like, in a variety of colors; if you attach all of these, your Beauty Bear will have a glorious wreath!

FLOWER PETALS

With US H-8 (5mm) crochet hook and yarn C: Ch5. Join with sl st to form ring.

Round 1: 10sc into the center of ring. Join with sl st to the first st.

Round 2: *Work into the next sc [1sc, 3dc, 1sc], skip 1sc* rep. to the end of the round. (5 petals total). Join with sl st to first sc of first petal. Fasten off.

FLOWER CENTER

With US H-8 (5mm) crochet hook and yarn D: Ch3. Join with sl st to form ring.

Round 1: 10sc into the center of ring. Join with sl st to the first st. Fasten off.

LEAVES (MAKE 2)

With US H-8 (5mm) crochet hook and yarn E: Ch10, sl st into second ch from hook, work 1sc into each of the next 2ch, work 1hdc into each of the next 2ch, work 1dc into each of the next 2ch, ch2, sl st into the last ch. Fasten off.

Finishing

1 Sew the ears to the hat in the position shown on pages 72-73 using an invisible seam.
2 Sew the flower center to the flower.
3 Sew the leaves to the flower.
4 Sew the flower onto the hat.
5 Weave in ends.

MITTENS
(make 2)

With US 9 (5.5mm) double-pointed needles and yarn B, cast on 22 (24, 26) sts. Join to work in the round.

CUFF
Rounds 1-10 (1-12, 1-14): Work in k1, p1 rib.

THUMB GUSSET
Fasten off yarn B. Join in yarn A.
Round 11 (13, 15): M1, knit to end of round. 23 (25, 27) sts.
Round 12 (14, 16) and each alt round: Knit.
Round 13 (15, 17): M1, k3, m1, k20 (22, 24). 25 (27, 29) sts.
Round 15 (17, 19): M1, k5, m1, k20 (22, 24). 27 (29, 31) sts.
Round 17 (19, 21): M1, k7, m1, k20 (22, 24). 29 (31, 33) sts.
Round 18 (20, 22): Knit.

12-24 months and 2-3 years:
Round (21, 23): M1, k9, m1, k (22, 24). (33, 35) sts.

All sizes:
Round 19 (22, 24): K1, place 7 (9, 9) on waste yarn. Rejoin to work hand stitches in the round, k21 (23, 25). 22 (24, 26) sts.

HAND
Rounds 20-32 (23-38, 25-42): Knit.
Round 33 (39, 43): [K2tog] to end of round. 11 (12, 13) sts.
Round 34 (40, 44): Knit.
Round 35 (41, 45): [K2tog] 5 (6, 6) times, K1 (0, 1). 6 (6, 7) sts.
Cut yarn, thread through remaining stitches, and draw tight.

THUMB
Transfer 7 (9, 9) sts from waste yarn onto needles. Rejoin yarn A, pick up and knit 1 st. 8 (10, 10) sts. Join to work in the round.
Rounds 1-6 (1-6, 1-8): Knit.
Round 7 (7, 9): [K2tog] to end of round. 4 (5, 5) sts.
Finish as for mitten Hand.

Finishing
Weave in ends.

The two-color mittens complement the hat perfectly. You could add a flower decoration to the mittens as well.

birthday bear

This celebration bear project comes with its own party hat! The hat is stuffed to make it stand up, and topped with a cheerful pompom. Matching crocheted spots on the party hat and neck ruff complete the festive look.

Materials

Coverall hat and mittens

LEVEL: intermediate

SIZES
6-12 months (12-24 months, 2-3 years)

Finished measurements
From "cheek to cheek" around the hat: 14½ (15, 15½)in (37 [38, 39]cm)
Mitten circumference: 5½ (6, 6) in (14 [15, 15]cm)
Mitten length: 5½ (6½, 7½)in (14 [16.5, 19]cm)

Gauge
14 sts and 19 rows = 4in (10cm) square in stockinette stitch worked with US 10 (6mm) needles
15 sts and 19 rows = 4in (10cm) square in k1, p1 rib slightly stretched, worked with US 10 (6mm) needles

HAT

Yarn:
Color A: 1 x 3.5oz (100g) ball (120yd/109m) Patons Classic Wool Roving Yarn, 100% pure new wool, Natural
Color B: 1 x 3.5oz (100g) ball (120yd/109m) Patons Classic Wool Roving Yarn, 100% pure new wool, Aran

Small amount:
Color C: Patons Classic Wool Roving Yarn, 100% pure new wool, Cherry

Equipment:
- US 10 (6mm) circular needle
- 1 pair of US 10 (6mm) needles
- US H-8 (5mm) crochet hook
- Optional: Stitch marker to indicate the start of a round
- Yarn needle
- Stuffing
- Two circles of cardboard 1½in (3.5cm) in diameter or a pompom maker

MITTENS

Yarn:
Color A: Patons Classic Wool Roving Yarn, 100% pure new wool, Natural

Small amounts:
Color B: Patons Classic Wool Roving Yarn, 100% pure new wool, Aran

Equipment:
- 4 x US 10 (6mm) double-pointed needles
- Optional: Stitch marker to indicate the start of a round
- Yarn needle

HAT

With a US 10 (6mm) circular needle and yarn A, cast on 52 (54, 56) sts. Join to work in the round.

Rounds 1-6 (1-6, 1-6): Work in k1, p1, rib.

Work in rows.

Row 7 (7, 7): K45 (47, 49), place next 7 (7, 7) stitches on waste yarn, turn. 45 (47, 49) sts.

Rows 8-24 (8-26, 8-28): Work in stockinette stitch pattern set.

Work short rows.

Row 25 (27, 29): K14 (15, 15), k2tog, k13 (13, 15), k2tog, turn. 43 (45, 47) sts.

Row 26 (28, 30): Sl1, p13 (13, 15), p2tog, turn. 42 (44, 46) sts.

Make sure you position the party hat at an angle just to the side of the top center of the main hat.

Row 27 (29, 31): Sl1, k13 (13, 15), k2tog, turn. 41 (43, 45) sts.

Rows 28-51 (30-55, 32-57): Rep. last 2 rows 12 (13, 13) times. 17 (17, 19) sts.

Row 52 (56, 58): Rep. row 26 (28, 30) once. 16 (16, 18) sts.

NECK RUFF

With a US 10 (6mm) circular needle, work in the round.

Fasten off yarn A. Join in yarn B.

Round 53 (57, 59): Sl1, k13 (13, 15), k2tog, pick up and knit 10 (11, 11), along edge, k7 (7, 7) stitches from waste yarn, pick up and knit 10 (11, 11) along edge. 42 (44, 46) sts.

Rounds 54-60 (58-66, 60-70): Knit.

Round 61 (67, 71): K1 (2, 3), m1, [k4 (4, 4), m1] 10 (10, 10) times, k1 (2, 3). 53 (55, 57) sts.

Round 62 (68, 72): Knit.

Round 63 (69, 73): K2 (3, 4), m1, [K5 (5, 5), m1] 10 (10, 10) times, k1 (2, 3). 64 (66, 68) sts.

Round 64 (70, 74): Knit.

Round 65 (71, 75): K3 (4, 5), m1, [k6 (6, 6), m1] 10 (10, 10) times, k1 (2, 3). 75 (77, 79) sts.

The birthday bear's neat little ears curl naturally when they are sewn onto the hat.

Round 66 (72, 76): Knit.
Round 67 (73, 77): K4 (5, 6), m1, [k7 (7, 7), m1] 10 (10, 10) times, k1 (2, 3). 86 (88, 90) sts.
Round 68 (74, 78): Knit.
Round 69 (75, 79): K5 (6, 7), m1, [k8 (8, 8), m1] 10 (10, 10) times, k1 (2, 3). 97 (99, 101) sts.

6-12 months:
Round 70: K2tog, k to end of round. 96 sts.

12-24 months and 2-3 years:
Round (76, 80): Knit.
Round (77, 81): K (7, 8), m1, [k (9, 9), m1] (10, 10) times, k (2, 3). (110, 112) sts.
Round (78, 82): Knit.

2-3 years:
Round (83): K9, m1, [K10, m1] 10 times, k3. (123) sts.
Round (84): K2tog, knit to end of round. (122) sts.

All sizes:
Rounds 71-76 (79-84, 85-90): Work in k1, p1, rib. 96 (110, 122) sts. Bind off.

EARS
(make 2)
With US 10 (6mm) straight needles and yarn A, cast on 20 sts.
Rows 1-5: Work in k1, p1, rib. Cut yarn, thread through remaining stitches, and draw tight.

Here you can see the position of the party hat in relation to the ear. Make sure the spots are facing the front.

PARTY HAT
With US 10 (6mm) double-pointed needles and yarn B, cast on 27 sts. Join to work in the round.
Rounds 1–2: Knit.
Round 3: [K2tog, k7] 3 times. 24 sts.
Rounds 4–5: Knit.
Round 6: [K2tog, k6] 3 times. 21 sts.
Rounds 7–8: Knit.
Round 9: [K2tog, k5] 3 times. 18 sts.
Rounds 10–11: Knit.
Round 12: [K2tog, k4] 3 times. 15 sts.

Rounds 13–14: Knit.
Round 15: [K2tog, k3] 3 times. 12 sts.
Rounds 16–17: Knit.
Round 18: [K2tog, k2] 3 times. 9 sts.
Rounds 19–20: Knit.
Round 21: [K2tog, k1] 3 times. 6 sts.
Round 22: Knit.
Cut yarn, thread through remaining stitches, and draw tight.

POMPOMS
Using two circles of cardboard 1½in (3.5cm) in diameter or a pompom maker, make one pompom in yarn C.

SPOTS (MAKE 5)
With US H-8 (5mm) crochet hook and C: Ch3. Join with sl st to form ring.
Round 1: 7sc into the center of ring. Join with sl st to the first st. Fasten off.

Finishing
1   Sew the ears onto the hat.
2   Sew the pompom onto the party hat.
3   Sew 2 spots onto the party hat.
4   Sew 3 spots onto the front of the neck ruff.
5   Stuff the party hat.
6   Sew the party hat onto the hat.
7   Weave in ends.

MITTENS
(make 2)

With US 10 (6mm) double-pointed needles and B, cast on 32 (36, 36) sts. Join to work in the round.

CUFF
Rounds 1-4 (1-5, 1-6): Work in p1, k1, rib.
Fasten off yarn B. Join in yarn A.
Round 5 (6, 7): [K2tog] 16 (18, 18) times. 16 (18, 18) sts.
Rounds 6-11 (7-13, 8-15): Work in k1, p1, rib.
Round 12 (14, 16): Knit.

THUMB GUSSET
Round 13 (15, 17): K7 (8, 8), m1, k2 (2, 2), m1, k7 (8, 8). 18 (20, 20) sts.
Round 14 (16, 18): Knit.
Round 15 (17, 19): K7 (8, 8), m1, k4 (4, 4), m1, k7 (8, 8). 20 (22, 22) sts.
Round 16 (18, 20): Knit.
Round 17 (19, 21): K7 (8, 8), m1, k6 (6, 6), m1, k7 (8, 8). 22 (24, 24) sts.
Round 18 (20, 22): Knit.

12-24 months and 2-3 years:
Round (21, 23): K (8, 8), m1, k (8, 8), m1, k (8, 8). (26, 26) sts.
Round (22, 24): Knit.

All sizes:
Round 19 (23, 25): K8 (9, 9), place 6 (8, 8) thumb stitches on waste yarn. Rejoin to work hand stitches in the round, k8 (9, 9). 16 (18, 18) sts.

HAND
Rounds 20-29 (24-34, 26-38): Knit.
Round 30 (35, 39): [K2tog] to end of round. 8 (9, 9) sts.

Round 31 (36, 40): Knit.
Round 32 (37, 41): [K2tog] 4 (4, 4) times, K0 (1, 1). 4 (5, 5) sts.
Cut yarn, thread through remaining stitches, and draw tight.

THUMB
Transfer 6 (8, 8) stitches from waste yarn onto needles. Rejoin yarn and pick up and knit 1 st. 7 (9, 9) sts. Join to work in the round.
Rounds 1-4 (1-5, 1-5): Knit.
Round 5 (6, 6): [K2tog] 3 (4, 4) times, K1 (1, 1). 4 (5, 5) sts.
Finish as for mitten Hand.

Finishing
Weave in ends.

The cozy mittens are gathered in at the wrists and have long cuffs for extra warmth.

cuddly koala

Boucle yarn creates the effect of soft koala fur for the hat, mittens, and leg warmers. Fluffy ears from Fun Fur Exotics yarn and the crocheted ears and nose make this koala truly lifelike.

Materials

Coverall hat, mittens, and leg warmers

LEVEL: intermediate

SIZES
6-12 months (12-24 months, 2-3 years)

Finished measurements
From "cheek to cheek" around the hat: 15 (15½, 16)in (38 [39.5, 40.5]cm)
Mitten circumference: 5½ (6, 6½)in (13.75 [15, 16.25]cm)
Mitten length: 5½ (6½, 7)in (14 [16.5, 18]cm)
Leg-warmer circumference: 8 (8½, 9)in (20 [21.5, 23]cm)
Leg-warmer length: 8 (9, 10)in (20 [23, 25.5]cm)

Gauge
15 sts and 20 rows = 4in (10cm) square in stockinette stitch worked with US 7 (4.5 mm) needles
16 sts and 20 rows = 4in (10cm) square in k1, p1 rib unstretched worked with US 7 (4.5 mm) needles

HAT

Yarn:
Color A: 1 x 5oz (140g) ball (255yd/233m) Bernat Soft Boucle Yarn, 97% acrylic, 3% polyester, Gray Shades

Small amounts:
Color B: Lion Brand Fun Fur Exotics Yarn, 100% polyester, Silver Fox
Color C: Lion Brand Jiffy Yarn, 100% acrylic, Black
Color D: Lion Brand Jiffy Yarn, 100% acrylic, White

Equipment:
- 1 pair of US 7 (4.5 mm) needles
- US 7 (4.5 mm) circular needle
- US H-8 (5mm) crochet hook
- Optional: Stitch marker to indicate the start of a round
- Yarn needle

MITTENS

Yarn:
Color A: 1 x 5oz (140g) ball (255yd/233m) Bernat Soft Boucle Yarn, 97% acrylic, 3% polyester, Gray Shades

Small amount:
Color B: Lion Brand Jiffy Yarn, 100% acrylic, Black

Equipment:
- 4 x US 7 (4.5 mm) double-pointed needles
- Optional: Stitch marker to indicate the start of a round
- Yarn needle

LEG WARMERS

Yarn:
Color A: As mittens

Small amount:
Color C: As mittens

Equipment:
As mittens

HAT

With a US 7 (4.5 mm) circular needle and yarn A, cast on 56 (60, 64) sts. Join to work in the round.

Rounds 1-6 (6, 6): Work in k1, p1, rib.

Work in rows.

Row 1 (1, 1): K 49 (53, 57), place next 7 (7, 7) sts onto waste yarn, turn. 49 (53, 57) sts.

Rows 2-26 (2-28, 2-30): Work in stockinette stitch.

Work in short rows.

Row 27 (29, 31): K15 (17, 18), k2tog, k15 (15, 17), k2tog, turn. 47 (51, 55) sts.

Row 28 (30, 32): Sl1, p15 (15, 17), p2tog, turn. 46 (50, 54) sts.

Row 29 (31, 33): Sl1, k15 (15, 17), k2tog, turn. 45 (49, 53) sts.

Rows 30-43 (32-49, 34-53): Rep. last 2 rows 7 (9, 10) times. 31 (31, 33) sts.

Row 44 (50, 54): Rep. row 28 (30, 31) once. 30 (30, 32) sts.

Row 45 (51, 55): Sl1, [p1, k1] 7 (7, 8) times, p1, k2tog, turn. 29 (29, 31) sts.

Row 46 (52, 56): Sl1, [k1, p1] 7 (7, 8) times, k1, p2tog, turn. 28 (28, 30) sts.

Rows 47-57 (53-62, 57-66): Rep. last 2 rows 5 (5, 5) times. 18 (18, 20) sts.

NECK RUFF

Work in the round.

Round 57 (63, 67): Sl1, [p1, k1] 7 (7, 8) times, p1, k2tog, pick up and knit 11 (11, 13) sts along edge, from waste yarn [k1, p1] 3 (3, 3) times, k1, pick up and knit 11 (11, 13) sts along edge. 46 (46, 52) sts.

Rounds 58-67 (64-75, 68-81): Work in k1, p1, rib.

Round 68 (76, 82): K2 (2, 2), yo, k2, yo, k9 (9, 11), yo, k2, yo, k10 (10, 11), yo, k2, yo, k9 (9, 11), yo, k2, yo, k8 (8, 9). 54 (54, 60) sts.

Round 69 (77, 83): K3 (3, 3), yo, k2, yo, k11 (11, 13), yo, k2, yo, k12 (12, 13), yo, k2, yo, k11 (11, 13), yo, k2, yo, k9 (9, 10). 62 (62, 68) sts.

Round 70 (78, 84): K4 (4, 4), yo, k2, yo, k13 (13, 15), yo, k2, yo, k14 (14, 15), yo, k2, yo, k13 (13, 15), yo, k2, yo, k10 (10, 11). 70 (70, 76) sts.

Round 71-72 (79-80, 85-86): Continue in increase pattern set. 86 (86, 92) sts.

2-3 years:

Round 87: Continue in increase pattern set. 100 sts.

All sizes:

Rounds 73-78 (81-86, 88-93): Work in k1, p1, rib. 86 (86, 100) sts. Bind off.

EARS

(make 2)

With US 7 (4.5 mm) straight needles and yarn B, cast on 25 sts. Fasten off yarn B. Join in yarn A.

Rows 1-7: Work in k1, p1, rib.

Cut yarn, thread through remaining stitches, and draw tight.

NOSE

With US H-8 (5mm) crochet hook and yarn C: Ch5. Join with sl st to form ring.

Round 1: Ch3, into the center of ring work [4dc, 4tr, 4dc, 4tr]. Join with sl st to top of beg-ch. Fasten off.

EYES

With US H-8 (5mm) crochet hook and C: ch3. Join with sl st to form ring.

Round 1: 7sc into the center of ring. Join with sl st to the first st. Fasten off.

Finishing

1   Fold the ears to mirror each other, folding one side of the ear to the middle of the ear.

2   Sew the ears to the hat in position shown using an invisible seam. The folded sides will face toward the front of the hat. The folded sides should be facing each other.

3   Sew the nose to the hat in position shown using an invisible seam.

4   Sew the eyes onto the hat.

5   With yarn D, embroider two small highlights in satin stitch.

6   Weave in ends.

MITTENS
(make 2)
With US 7 (4.5 mm) double-pointed needles and yarn B, cast on 22 (24, 26) sts. Join to work in the round.

CUFF
Rounds 1-10 (1-12, 1-14): Work in Work in k1, p1, rib.

THUMB GUSSET
Fasten off yarn B. Join in yarn A.
Round 11 (13, 15): M1R, k to end of round. 23 (25, 27) sts.
Round 12 (14, 16) and each alt round: Knit.
Round 13 (15, 17): M1R, k1, M1L, k to end of round. 25 (27, 29) sts.
Round 15 (17, 19): M1R, k3, M1L, k to end of round. 27 (29, 31) sts.
Round 17 (19, 21): M1R, k5, M1L, k to end of round. 29 (31, 33) sts.
Round 18 (20, 22): Knit.

12-24 months and 2-3 years:
Round (21, 23): M1R, k7, M1L, k to end of round. (33, 35) sts.

All sizes:
Round 19 (22, 24): K1, place 7 (9, 9) on waste yarn. Rejoin to work hand stitches in the round, k21 (23, 25). 22 (24, 26) sts.

HAND
Rounds 20-32 (23-38, 25-42): Knit.
Round 33 (39, 43): [K2tog] to end of round. 11 (12, 13) sts.
Round 34 (40, 44): Knit.
Round 35 (41, 45): [K2tog] 5 (6, 6) times, K1 (0, 1). 6 (6, 7) sts.

Cut yarn, thread through remaining stitches, and draw tight.

THUMB
Transfer 7 (9, 9) sts from waste yarn onto needles. Rejoin yarn A, pick up and knit 1 st. 8 (10, 10) sts. Join to work in the round.
Rounds 1-6 (1-6, 1-8): Knit.
Round 7 (7, 9): [K2tog] to end of round. 4 (5, 5) sts.
Finish as for mitten Hand.

Finishing
Weave in ends.

LEG WARMERS
(make 2)
With US 7 (4.5 mm) double-pointed needles and yarn C, cast on 32 (34, 36) sts. Join to work in the round.

Cozy koala mittens and leg warmers—the leg warmers are particularly quick and easy to make.

CUFF
Rounds 1-6 (1-6, 1-6): Work in k1, p1, rib.
Fasten off yarn C. Join in yarn A.

LEG
Rounds 7-36 (7-43, 7-51): Knit.
Fasten off yarn A. Join in yarn C.
Round 37 (44, 52): Knit.

CUFF
Rounds 38-45 (45-52, 53-60): Work in k1, p1, rib.
Bind off.

Finishing
Weave in ends.

polar bear

The cable technique is used to achieve the special texture on this hat, while the mittens are made in a stretchy rib stitch to ensure a good fit. If you are new to cabling, see page 132 for full instructions.

Coverall hat and mittens

LEVEL: intermediate

SIZES
6-12 months (12-24 months, 2-3 years)

Finished measurements
From "cheek to cheek" around the hat: 14½ (15, 15½)in (37 [38, 39]cm)
Mitten circumference: 5½ (6, 6) in (14 [15, 15]cm)
Mitten length: 5½ (6½, 7½)in (14 [16.5, 19]cm)

Gauge
14 sts and 19 rows = 4in (10cm) square-in stockinette stitch worked with US 10 (6mm) needles
15 sts and 19 rows = 4in (10cm) square in k1, p1 rib unstretched, worked with US 10 (6mm) needles

Materials

HAT

Yarn:
1 x 3.5oz (100g) ball (120yd/109m) Bernat Roving, 80% acrylic, 20% wool, Rice Paper

Equipment:
- US 10 (6mm) circular needle
- 1 pair of US 10 (6mm) needles
- Optional: Stitch marker to indicate the start of a round
- Cable needle
- Yarn needle

MITTENS

Yarn:
1 x 3.5oz (100g) ball (120yd/109m) Bernat Roving, 80% acrylic, 20% wool, Rice Paper

Equipment:
- 4 x US 10 (6mm) double-pointed needles
- Optional: Stitch marker to indicate the start of a round
- Yarn needle

HAT

With a US 10 (6mm) circular needle, cast on 52 (54, 56) sts. Join to work in the round.

Rounds 1-4 (1-4, 1-4): Work in k1, p1, rib.

Work in rows.

Row 5 (5, 5): *[K1, p1] 4 times, m1 * rep. from * to * 5 times, [K1, p1] 2 (3, 4) times, k1, place next 7 stitches on waste yarn, turn. 50 (52, 54) sts.

Row 6 (6, 6): P2 (3, 4), k2, [p4, k2] 3 times, p6, [k2, p4] 3 times, k2, p2 (3, 4). 50 (52, 54) sts.

Row 7 (7, 7): K2 (3, 4), p2, sl next stitch to cn and hold in back, k1, k1 from cn, sl next stitch to cn and hold in front, k1, k1 from cn, p2, sl next 2 sts to cn and hold in back, k2, k2 from cn, p2, sl next 3 sts to cn and hold in back, k1, k3 from cn, p2, sl next 2 sts to cn and hold in back, k1, k2 from cn, sl next stitch to cn and hold in front, k2, k1 from cn, p2, sl next stitch to cn and hold in front, k3, k1 from cn, p2, sl next 2 sts to cn and hold in front, k2, k2 from cn, p2, sl next stitch to cn and hold in back, k1, k1 from cn, sl next stitch to cn and hold in front, k1, k1 from cn, p2, k2 (3, 4). 50 (52, 54) sts.

Row 8 (8, 8): Rep. row 6 (6, 6).

Row 9 (9, 9): K2 (3, 4), p2, [k4, p2] 3 times, k6, [p2, k4] 3 times, p2, k2 (3, 4). 50 (52, 54) sts.

Row 10-17 (10-21, 10-21): Rep. rows 6-9 (6-9, 6-9) 2 (3, 3) times.

Rows 18-19 (22-23, 22-23): Rep. rows 6-7 (6-7, 6-7) once.

Row 20 (24, 24): P2 (3, 4), k2, p1, p2tog, p1, k2, p2, p2tog, k2, p4, k2, p6, [k2, p4] 3 times, k2, p2 (3, 4). 48 (50, 52) sts.

Work short rows.

Row 21 (25, 25): K2 (3, 4), p2, k1, k2tog, k1, p2, k2, k2tog, p1, k2tog, k3, p2, k6, p2, k3, k2tog, turn. 44 (46, 48) sts.

Row 22 (26, 26): Sl1, p3, k2, p6, k2, p3, p2tog, turn. 43 (45, 47).

Row 23 (27, 27): Sl1, sl next 2 sts to cn and hold in back, k1, k2 from

Here you can see how the cables look close up; note the position of the ear over the cabled section.

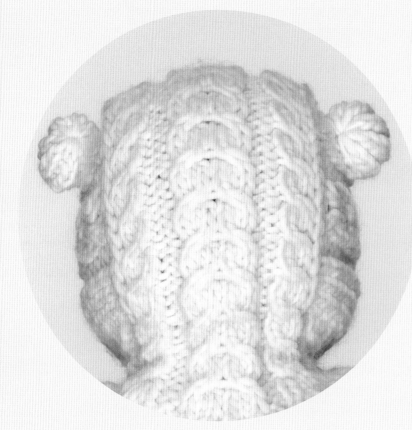

The pattern continues neatly down the back of the hat and to the neck ruff, so it feels smooth to the wearer.

cn, p2, sl next 2 sts to cn and hold in back, k1, k2 from cn, sl next stitch to cn and hold in front, k2, k1, from cn, p2, sl next stitch to cn and hold in front, k2, k1 from cn, k2tog, turn. 42 (44, 46) sts.

Row 24 (28, 28): Rep. row 22 (26, 26). 41 (43, 45) sts.

Row 25 (29, 29): Sl1, k3, p2, k6, p2, k3, k2tog, turn. 40 (42, 44) sts.

Row 26 (30, 30): Rep. row 22 (26, 26). 39 (41, 43) sts.

Row 27 (31, 31): Rep. row 23 (27, 27). 38 (40, 42) sts.

Row 28 (32, 32): Rep. row 22 (26, 26). 37 (39, 41) sts.

Row 29 (33, 33): Rep. row 25 (29, 29). 36 (38, 40) sts.

Rows 30-45 (34-49, 34-53): Rep. rows 26-29 (30-33, 30-33) 4 (4, 5) times. 20 (22, 20) sts.

6-12 months:
Row 46: Rep. row 26. 19 sts.

12-24 months:
Rows 50-52: Rep. rows 30-32 once. 19 sts.

2-3 years:
Row 54: Rep. row 30 once. 19 sts.

NECK RUFF
Work in the round.

6-12 months:
Round 47: Sl1, sl next 2 sts to cn and hold in back, k1, k2 from cn, p2, sl next 2 sts to cn and hold in back, k1, k2 from cn, sl next stitch to cn and hold in front, k2, k1 from cn, p2, sl next stitch to cn and hold in front, k2, k1 from cn, k2tog, pick up and knit 8 stitches along edge, from waste yarn [p1, k1] 3 times, p1, pick up and knit 8 stitches along edge. 41 sts.

Rounds 48-50: P1, k3, p2, k6, p2, [k3, p1] twice, k3, p2, k5, p2, k3, p1, k3. 41 sts.

Round 51: P1, sl next 2 sts to cn and hold in back, k1, k2 from cn, p2, sl next 2 sts to cn and hold in back, k1, k2 from cn, sl next stitch to cn and hold in front, k2, k1 from cn, p2, *sl next stitch to cn and hold in front, k2, k1 from cn, p1, * rep. from * to * 3 times, p1, sl next stitch to cn and hold in back, k1, k1 from cn, k1, sl next stitch to cn and hold in front, k1, k1 from cn, p2, sl next 2 sts to cn and hold in back, k1, k2 from cn, p1, sl next 2 sts to cn and hold in back, k1, k2 from cn. 41 sts.
Rounds 52-54: Rep. round 48.
Round 55: Rep. round 51.
Round 56: [K3, m1] 13 times, k2, m1. 55 sts.
Rounds 57-62: Work in k1, p1, rib. Bind off.

12-24 months:

Round 53: Sl1, k3, p2, k6, p2, k3, k2tog, pick up and knit 10 stitches along edge, from waste yarn [p1, k1] 3 times, p1, pick up and knit 10 stitches along edge. 45 sts.
Round 54: P1, k3, p2, k6, [p2, k3] 3 times, p2, k5, p2, k3, p2, k3, p1. 45 sts.
Round 55: P1, sl next 2 sts to cn and hold in back, k1, k2 from cn, p2, sl next 2 sts to cn and hold in back, k1, k2 from cn, *sl next stitch to cn and hold in front, k2, k1 from cn, p2,* rep. from * to * 4 times, sl next stitch to cn and hold in back, k1, k1 from cn, k1, sl next stitch to cn and hold in front, k1, k1 from cn, p2, sl next 2 sts to cn and hold in back, k1, k2 from cn, p2, sl next 2 sts to cn and hold in back, k1, k2 from cn, p1. 45 sts.
Rounds 56-58: Rep. round 54.
Round 59: Rep. round 55.

Rounds 60-61: Rep. round 54, 56.
Round 62: [K3, m1] 15 times. (60, 60) sts.
Rounds 63-68: Work in k1, p1, rib. Bind off.

2-3 years:

Round 55: Sl1, sl next 2 sts to cn and hold in back, k1, k2 from cn, p2, sl next 2 sts to cn and hold in back, k1, k2 from cn, sl next stitch to cn and hold in front, k2, k1 from cn, p2, sl next stitch to cn and hold in front, k2, k1 from cn, k2tog, pick up and knit 10 stitches along edge, from waste yarn [p1, k1] 3 times, p1, pick up and knit 10 stitches along edge. 45 sts.
Rounds 56-58: P1, k3, p2, k6, [p2, k3] 3 times, p2, k5, p2, k3, p2, k3, p1. 45 sts.
Round 59: P1, sl next 2 sts to cn and hold in back, k1, k2 from cn, p2, sl next 2 sts to cn and hold in back, k1, k2 from cn, *sl next stitch to cn and hold in front, k2, k1 from cn, p2,* rep. from * to * 4 times, sl next stitch to cn and hold in back, k1, k1 from cn, k1, sl next stitch to cn and hold in front, k1, k1 from cn, p2, sl next 2 sts to cn and hold in back, k1, k2 from cn, p2, sl next 2 sts to cn and hold in back, k1, k2 from cn, p1. 45 sts.

Rounds 60-62: Rep. round 56.
Round 63: Rep. round 59.
Rounds 64-65: Rep. round 56.
Round 66: [K3, m1] 15 times. 60 sts.
Rounds 67-72: Work in k1, p1, rib. Bind off.

EARS
(make 2)
With US 10 (6mm) straight needles, cast on 13 sts.
Rows 1-4: Work in k1, p1, rib. Cut yarn, thread through remaining stitches, and draw tight.

Finishing
1 Sew the ears onto the hat.
2 Weave in ends.

MITTENS
(make 2)

With US 10 (6mm) double-pointed needles cast on 16 (18, 18) sts. Join to work in the round.

CUFF
Rounds 1-12 (1-13, 1-14): Work in k1, p1, rib.

THUMB BASE
Round 13 (14, 15): [K1, p1] 3 times, k1, place next 4 stitches on waste yarn, cast on 4 stitches (right-hand needle), rejoin to work hand stitches in the round, [p1, k1] 2 (3, 3) times, p1. 16 (18, 18) sts.

HAND
Rounds 14-22 (15-24, 16-27): Work in k1, p1, rib.
Round 23 (25, 28): [K2tog] to end of round. 8 (9, 9) sts.

Round 24 (26, 29): Knit.
Round 25 (27, 30): [K2tog] 4 (4, 4) times, KO (1, 1). 4 (5, 5) sts.
Cut yarn, thread through remaining stitches, and draw tight.

THUMB
Transfer 4 stitches from waste yarn onto needles, pick up and knit 4 sts across the 4 cast-on sts. 8 (8, 8) sts.
Rounds 1-6 (1-7, 1-8): Knit.
Round 7 (8, 9): [K2tog] to end of round. 4 (4, 4) sts.
Finish as for mitten Hand.

Finishing
Weave in ends.

In contrast to the cables on the hat, the mittens are mostly knitted in a rib pattern.

fantasy
friends

friendly monster

This gentle monster is sure to inspire many imaginative games. The pattern is quite simple—the hat, mittens, and booties are knitted in garter and stockinette stitch. The little horns should stick upright without stuffing.

Coverall hat, mittens, and booties

LEVEL: beginner

SIZES
6-12 months (12-24 months, 2-3 years)

Finished measurements
From "cheek to cheek" around the hat: 14½ (15, 15½)in (37 [38, 39]cm)
Mitten circumference: 5½ (6, 6) in (14 [15, 15]cm)
Mitten length: 5½ (6½, 7½)in (14 [16.5, 19]cm)

Gauge
14 sts and 28 rows = 4in (10cm) square in garter stitch worked with US 10 (6mm) needles
14 sts and 19 rows = 4in (10cm) square in stockinette stitch worked with US 10 (6mm) needles
15 sts and 19 rows = 4in (10cm) square in k1, p1 rib slightly stretched, worked with US 10 (6mm) needles

Materials

HAT

Main yarn:
Color A: 1 x 3.5oz (100g) ball (120yd/109m) Patons Classic Wool Roving, 100% Pure New Wool, Taupe

Small amounts:
Color B: Patons Classic Wool Roving, 100% Pure New Wool, Pumpkin
Color C: Patons Classic Wool Roving, 100% Pure New Wool, Yellow

Equipment:
- US 10 (6mm) circular needle
- 1 pair of US 9 (5.5mm) double-pointed needles
- Optional: Stitch marker to indicate the start of a round
- Yarn needle

FINGERLESS MITTENS

Main yarn:
Color A: 1 x 3.5oz (100g) ball (120yd/109m) Patons Classic Wool Roving, 100% Pure New Wool, Taupe

Small amounts:
Color B: Patons Classic Wool Roving, 100% Pure New Wool, Pumpkin
Color C: Patons Classic Wool Roving, 100% Pure New Wool, Yellow

Equipment:
- 4 x US 10 (6mm) double-pointed needles
- Stitch marker
- Yarn needle

BOOTIES

Yarn:
Color A: As mittens

Small amounts:
Color B: As mittens
Color C: As mittens

Equipment:
As mittens

HAT

With a US 10 (6mm) circular needle and yarn A, cast on 52 (54, 56) sts.

Join to work in the round.

Round 1 (1, 1): Work in k1, p1, rib.

Round 2 (2, 2): Knit.

Rounds 3-5 (3-5, 3-5): Rep. rounds 1-2 once, and round 1 once more.

Work in rows.

Row 6 (6, 6): K45 (47, 49), place next 7 (7, 7) stitches on waste yarn, turn. 45 (47, 49) sts.

Rows 7-31 (7-33, 7-35): Work in garter stitch.

Work short rows.

Row 32 (34, 36): K14 (14, 15), k2tog, k13 (15, 15), k2tog, turn. 43 (45, 47) sts.

Row 33 (35, 37): K14 (16, 16), k2tog, turn. 42 (44, 46) sts.

Rows 34-59 (36-61, 38-65): Rep. the last row 26 (26, 28) times. 16 (18, 18) sts.

NECK RUFF

Work in the round.

Fasten off yarn A. Join in yarn B.

Round 60 (62, 66): K14 (16, 16), k2tog, pick up and knit 11 (12, 14) along edge, from waste yarn k7

(7, 7), pick up and knit 11 (12, 14) along edge. 44 (48, 52) sts.

Rounds 61-64 (63-67, 67-71): Knit.

Fasten off yarn B. Join in yarn C.

Rounds 65-69 (68-73, 72-77): Knit.

Fasten off yarn C. Join in yarn B.

Rounds 70-74 (74-79, 78-83): Knit.

Fasten off yarn B. Join in yarn C.

Round 75 (80, 84): [K4, m1] 10 (11, 12) times, k4. 54 (59, 64) sts.

Rounds 76-80 (81-85, 85-89): Work in k1, p1, rib.

Bind off.

HORNS

(make 2)

With US 8 (5mm) double-pointed needles and yarn C, cast on 12 sts. Join to work in the round.

Rounds 1-5: Knit.

Round 6: K1, k2tog, k2, k2tog, k2, k2tog, k1. 9 sts.

Rounds 7-8: Knit.

Round 9: [K1, k2tog] 3 times. 6 sts.

Rounds 10-11: Knit.

Round 12: [K2tog] 3 times. 3 sts. Cut yarn, thread through remaining stitches, and draw tight.

Finishing

1 Sew the horns onto the hat.
2 Weave in ends.

FINGERLESS MITTENS

(make 2)

With US 10 (6mm) double-pointed needles and yarn C, cast on 16 (18, 18) sts. Join to work in the round.

CUFF

Rounds 1-6 (1-6, 1-6): Work in k1, p1, rib.

Fasten off yarn C. Join in yarn A.

Round 7 (7, 7): Knit.

Round 8 (8, 8): Purl.

Rounds 9-16 (9-18, 9-18): Work in stockinette stitch.

THUMB GUSSET

Round 17 (19, 19): K8 (9, 9), m1, k8 (9, 9). 17 (19, 19) sts.

Round 18 (20, 20): Purl.

Round 19 (21, 21): K8 (9, 9), m1, k1 (1, 1), m1, k8 (9, 9). 19 (21, 21) sts.

Round 20 (22, 22): Purl.

Round 21 (23, 23): K8 (9, 9), m1, k3 (3, 3), m1, k8 (9, 9). 21 (23, 23) sts.

Round 22 (24, 24): Purl.

Round 23 (25, 25): Knit.

Round 24 (26, 26): P8 (9, 9), bind off 5 (5, 5) stitches, p8 (9, 9). 16 (18, 18) sts.

HAND

Fasten off yarn A. Join in yarn B.

Round 25 (27, 27): Knit.

Rounds 26-28 (28-30, 28-30): Work in k1, p1, rib.

Bind off.

Finishing

1 Weave in ends.

BOOTIES
(make 2)

With US 10 (6mm) double-pointed needles and yarn C, cast on 22 (24, 24) sts. Join to work in the round.
Rounds 1-6 (1-6, 1-6): Work in k1, p1, rib.
Fasten off yarn C. Join in yarn A.
Round 7 (7, 7): Knit.
Round 8 (8, 8): Purl.
Rounds 9-22 (9-24, 9-26): Work in stockinette stitch.
Round 23 (25, 27): *K3 (4, 4), k2tog, k4 (4, 4), k2tog* rep. from * to * twice. 18 (20, 20) sts.
Round 24 (26, 28): Purl.

HEEL
Work in rows.
Join in yarn B.
Row 25 (27, 29): K10 (11, 11), turn.
Row 26 (28, 30): P10 (11, 11), turn.
Rows 27-30 (29-32, 31-34): Rep. rows 25-26 (27-28, 29-30) twice.
Row 31 (33, 35): K2 (2, 2), k2tog, k2 (3, 3), k2tog, turn. 8 (9, 9) sts.
Row 32 (34, 36): Sl1, p2 (3, 3), p2tog, turn. 7 (8, 8) sts.
Row 33 (35, 37): Sl1, k2 (3, 3), k2tog, turn. 6 (7, 7) sts.
Row 34 (36, 38): Sl1, p2 (3, 3), p2tog, turn. 5 (6, 6) sts.
Work in rounds.
Round 35 (37, 39): Sl1, k2 (3, 3), k2tog, fasten off yarn B, using yarn A, pick up and knit 3 (3, 3) stitches down side of heel, k8 (9, 9), pick up and knit 3 (3, 3) stitches up side of heel, 18 (20, 20) sts.
Work the following partial round to the new starting position for the following rounds.

Round 36 (38, 40): k4 (5, 5), p11 (12, 12).
Place a marker at the beginning of the round.
Round 37 (39, 41): Knit.
Round 38 (40, 42): Purl.
Rounds 39-46 (41-50, 43-54): Rep. last 2 rounds 4 (5, 6) times. Fasten off yarn A. Join in yarn B.
Rounds 47-50 (51-54, 55-58): Knit.
Round 51 (55, 59): [K2tog] rep. to end of round. 9 (10, 10) sts.
Round 52 (56, 60): [K2tog] 4 (5, 5) times, K1 (0, 0). 5 (5, 5) sts.
Cut yarn, thread through remaining stitches, and draw tight.

The fingerless mittens have a thumb gusset for comfort and give little fingers freedom to move, and the booties are extremely warm.

Finishing
1 Weave in ends.

unique unicorn

This fun mythical creature has a splendid horn that is stuffed to keep it upright.
It's easy to create the appealing mane from lengths of gold-colored yarn. The
matching mittens are created in the same main color.

Coverall hat and mittens

LEVEL: intermediate

SIZES
6-12 months (12-24 months, 2-3 years)

Finished measurements
From "cheek to cheek" around the hat: 14½ (15, 15½)in (37 [38, 39]cm)
Mitten circumference: 5½ (6, 6) in (14 [15, 15]cm)
Mitten length: 5½ (6½, 7½)in (14 [16.5, 19]cm)

Gauge
14 sts and 19 rows = 4in (10cm) square in stockinette stitch worked with US 10 (6 mm) needles
15 sts and 19 rows = 4in (10cm) square in k1, p1 rib slightly stretched, worked with US 10 (6mm) needles

Materials

HAT

Yarn:
Color A: 2 x 3.5oz (100g) balls (120yd/109m) Patons Classic Wool Roving Yarn, 100% pure new wool, Aran
Color B: Patons Classic Wool Roving Yarn, 100% pure new wool, Yellow

Small amount:
Color C: Patons Classic Wool Roving Yarn, 100% pure new wool, Natural

Equipment:
- US 10 (6 mm) circular needle
- 1 pair of US 10 (6 mm) double-pointed needles
- US J-10 (6mm) crochet hook
- Optional: Stitch marker to indicate the start of a round
- Yarn needle
- Stuffing

MITTENS

Yarn:
Color A: 1 x 3.5oz (100g) ball (120yd/109m) Patons Classic Wool Roving Yarn, 100% pure new wool, Aran

Equipment:
- 4 x US 10 (6 mm) double-pointed needles
- Optional: Stitch marker to indicate the start of a round
- Yarn needle

HAT

With a US 10 (6 mm) circular needle and yarn A, cast on 52 (54, 56) sts. Join to work in the round.

Rounds 1-6 (1-6, 1-6): Work in k1, p1, rib.

Work in rows.

Row 7 (7, 7): K45 (47, 49), place next 7 (7, 7) stitches on waste yarn, turn. 45 (47, 49) sts.

Rows 8-14 (8-16, 8-16): Work in stockinette stitch pattern set.

EAR SHAPING

Row 15 (17, 17): K18 (19, 20), yo, k2, yo, k5, yo, k2, yo, k18 (19, 20). 49 (51, 53) sts.

Row 16 (18, 18): P19 (20, 21), yo, p2, yo, p7, yo, p2, yo, p19 (20, 21). 53 (55, 57) sts.

Row 17 (19, 19): K20 (21, 22), yo, k2, yo, k9, yo, k2, yo, k20 (21, 22). 57 (59, 61) sts.

Row 18 (20, 20): P21 (22, 23), yo, p2, yo, p11, yo, p2, yo, p21 (22, 23). 61 (63, 65) sts.

Row 19 (21, 21): K22 (23, 24), yo, k2, yo, k13, yo, k2, yo, k22 (23, 24). 65 (67, 69) sts.

Row 20 (22, 22): P23 (24, 25), yo, p2, yo, p15, yo, p2, yo, p23 (24, 25). 69 (71, 73) sts.

Row 21 (23, 23): K24 (25, 26), yo, k2, yo, k17, yo, k2, yo, k24 (25, 26). 73 (75, 77) sts.

Row 22 (24, 24): P25 (26, 27), yo, p2, yo, p19, yo, p2, yo, p25 (26, 27). 77 (79, 81) sts.

Row 23 (25, 25): K25 (26, 27), [k2tog] twice, turn, sl1, p2tog, turn, *sl1, k2tog, turn, sl1, p2tog, turn* rep. from * to * 6 (6, 6) times, sl1, k2tog, k12 (12, 12), [k2tog] twice, turn, sl1, p2tog, turn, **sl1, k2tog, turn, sl1, p2tog, turn** rep. from **

to ** 6 (6, 6) times, sl1, k2tog, k18 (19, 20). 45 (47, 49) sts.

Row 24 (26, 26): Purl.

2-3 years:

Rows 27-28: Work in stockinette stitch.

All sizes:

Work short rows.

Row 25 (27, 29): K14 (15, 15), k2tog, k13 (13, 15), k2tog, turn. 43 (45, 47) sts.

Row 26 (28, 30): Sl1, p13 (13, 15), p2tog, turn. 42 (44, 46).

Row 27 (29, 31): Sl1, k13 (13, 15), k2tog, turn. 41 (43, 45) sts.

The unicorn looks fabulous from the back with its fantastic fringes. The mane can be made with any color you like—or even a mix of several colors.

Rows 28-51 (30-55, 32-57): Rep. last 2 rows 12 (13, 13) times. 17 (17, 19) sts.
Row 52 (56, 58): Rep. row 26 (28, 30) once. 16 (16, 18) sts.

NECK RUFF
Work in the round.
Round 53 (57, 59): Sl1, k13 (13, 15), k2tog, pick up and knit 10 (11, 11) stitches along edge, from waste yarn k7 (7, 7) pick up and knit 10 (11, 11) stitches along edge. 42 (44, 46) sts.
Rounds 54-60 (58-66, 60-70): Knit.
Round 61 (67, 71): K1 (2, 3), m1, [k4 (4, 4), m1] 10 (10, 10) times, k1 (2, 3). 53 (55, 57) sts.
Round 62 (68, 72): Knit.
Round 63 (69, 73): K2 (3, 4), m1, [k5 (5, 5), m1] 10 (10, 10) times, k1 (2, 3). 64 (66, 68) sts.
Round 64 (70, 74): Knit.
Round 65 (71, 75): K3 (4, 5), m1, [k6 (6, 6), m1] 10 (10, 10) times, k1 (2, 3). 75 (77, 79) sts.

Round 66 (72, 76): Knit.
Round 67 (73, 77): K4 (5, 6), m1, [k7 (7, 7), m1] 10 (10, 10) times, k1 (2, 3). 86 (88, 90) sts.
Round 68 (74, 78): Knit.
Round 69 (75, 79): K5 (6, 7), m1, [k8 (8, 8), m1] 10 (10, 10) times, k1 (2, 3). 97 (99, 101) sts.

6-12 months:
Round 70: K2tog, knit to end of round. 96 sts.

12-24 months and 2-3 years:
Round (76, 80): Knit.
Round (77, 81): K (7, 8), m1, [k (9, 9), m1] (10, 10) times, k (2, 3). (110, 112) sts.
Round (78, 82): Knit.

2-3 years:
Round 83: K9, m1, [k10, m1] 10 times, k3. 123 sts.
Round 84: K2tog, knit to end of round. (122) sts.

All sizes:
Rounds 71-76 (79-84, 85-90): Work in k1, p1, rib.
Bind off.

You can vary the lengths of the mane strands or trim them if you would like a neater finish.

HORN

With US 10 (6 mm) double-pointed needles and yarn C, cast on 16 sts. Join to work in the round.

Rounds 1-3: Knit.
Round 4: [K2tog, k6] twice. 14 sts.
Rounds 5-6: Knit.
Round 7: [K5, k2tog] twice. 12 sts.
Rounds 8-9: Knit.
Round 10: [K2tog, k4] twice. 10 sts.
Rounds 11-12: Knit.
Round 13: [K3, k2tog] twice. 8 sts.
Rounds 14-15: Knit.
Round 16: [K2tog, k2] twice. 6 sts.
Rounds 17-18: Knit.
Round 19: [K2tog] 3 times. 3 sts.
Round 20: K3.

Cut yarn, thread through remaining stitches, and draw tight.

MANE

To make 22 (26, 29) fringes, cut yarn B to make 66 (78, 87) pieces, about 10-12in (25.5-30.5cm) long. Use 3 pieces of yarn to make 1 fringe. Gather 3 pieces of yarn together and fold them in half. Starting 6 rows from the rib:
*Insert J-10 (6mm) crochet hook into 23rd (24th, 25th) stitch (middle stitch in the row).
Insert J-10 (6mm) crochet hook into the loop of the folded-up pieces of yarn (as you insert the hook into the loop when crocheting a stitch).
Pull up the loop through the middle stitch.
Wrap the other side of the yarn pieces around your hook and pull everything through the loop.
Make it neater by pulling on the ends of the fringe and making sure the knot looks even and neat.
Skip one row. *
Rep. from * to * 22 (26, 29) times.

Finishing

1 Stuff the horn.
2 Sew the horn onto the hat.
3 Weave in ends.

The horn can be done in any color your little unicorn prefers! Use the photos to guide your horn placement.

MITTENS
(make 2)
With US 10 (6 mm) double-pointed needles and yarn A, cast on 32 (36, 36) sts. Join to work in the round.

CUFF
Rounds 1-4 (1-5, 1-6): P1, k1 rib.
Round 5 (6, 7): [K2tog] to the end of the round. 16 (18, 18) sts.
Rounds 6-11 (7-13, 8-15): Work in k1, p1, rib.
Round 12 (14, 16): Knit.

THUMB GUSSET
Round 13 (15, 17): K7 (8, 8), m1, k2 (2, 2), m1, k7 (8, 8). 18 (20, 20) sts.
Round 14 (16, 18): Knit.
Round 15 (17, 19): K7 (8, 8), m1, k4 (4, 4), m1, k7 (8, 8). 20 (22, 22) sts.
Round 16 (18, 20): Knit.
Round 17 (19, 21): K7 (8, 8), m1, k6 (6, 6), m1, k7 (8, 8). 22 (24, 24) sts.
Round 18 (20, 22): Knit.

12-24 months and 2-3 years:
Round (21, 23): K (8, 8), m1, k (8, 8), m1, k (8, 8). (26, 26) sts.
Round (22, 24): Knit.

All sizes:
Round 19 (23, 25): K8 (9, 9), place 6 (8, 8) thumb stitches on waste yarn. Rejoin to work hand stitches in the round, k8 (9, 9). 16 (18, 18) sts.

HAND
Rounds 20-29 (24-34, 26-38): Knit.
Round 30 (35, 39): [K2tog] to end of round. 8 (9, 9) sts.
Round 31 (36, 40): Knit.
Round 32 (37, 41): [K2tog] 4 (4, 4) times, k 0 (1, 1). 4 (5, 5) sts.
Cut yarn, thread through remaining stitches, and draw tight.

THUMB
Transfer 6 (8, 8) stitches from waste yarn onto needles. Rejoin yarn and pick up and knit 1 st. 7 (9, 9) sts.
Join to work in the round.
Rounds 1-4 (1-5, 1-5): Knit.
Round 5 (6, 6): [K2tog] 3 (4, 4) times, k1 (1, 1). 4 (5, 5) sts.
Finish as for mitten Hand.

Finishing
Weave in ends.

These classic mittens are made in the same neutral color as the hat.

chinese dragon

This extraordinary hat with impressive dragon features is straightforward to make. The horns are knitted, while the nose, nostrils, ears, and teeth are easy to crochet. The dragon eyes are also knitted into the mittens.

Coverall hat and mittens

LEVEL: advanced

SIZES
6-12 months (12-24 months, 2-3 years)

Finished measurements
From "cheek to cheek" around the hat: 14½ (15, 15½)in (37 [38, 39]cm)
Mitten circumference: 5½ (6, 6½)in (13.75 [15, 16.25]cm)
Mitten length: 5½ (6½, 7)in (14 [16.5, 18]cm)

Gauge
17 sts and 24 rows = 4in (10cm) square in stockinette stitch worked with US 8 (5mm) needles
19 sts and 24 rows = 4in (10cm) square in k1, p1 rib unstretched, worked with US 8 (5mm) needles.

Materials

HAT

Yarn:
Color A: 1 x 3oz (85g) ball (135yd/123m) Lion Brand Jiffy Yarn, 100% acrylic, True Red

Small amounts:
Color B: Lion Brand Jiffy Yarn, 100% acrylic, Gold
Color C: Lion Brand Jiffy Yarn, 100% acrylic, White
Color D: Lion Brand Jiffy Yarn, 100% acrylic, Black
Color E: Lion Brand Jiffy Yarn, 100% acrylic, Baby Blue

Equipment:
- 1 pair of US 8 (5mm) needles
- US 8 (5mm) circular needle
- 4 x US 8 (5mm) double-pointed needles
- US G-6 (4.25mm) crochet hook
- Optional: Stitch marker to indicate the start of a round
- Yarn needle

MITTENS

Yarn:
Color A: 1 x 3oz (85g) ball (135yd/123m) Lion Brand Jiffy Yarn, 100% acrylic, True Red

Small amounts:
Color C: Lion Brand Jiffy Yarn, 100% acrylic, White
Color D: Lion Brand Jiffy Yarn, 100% acrylic, Black
Color E: Lion Brand Jiffy Yarn, 100% acrylic, Baby Blue

Equipment:
- 4 x US 8 (5mm) double-pointed needles
- Optional: Stitch marker to indicate the start of a round
- Stitch holder
- Yarn needle

HAT

With US 8 (5mm) straight needles and A, cast on 57 (61, 65) sts.
Rows 1-6 (1-6, 1-6): Work in k1, p1, rib.
Rows 7-30 (7-30, 7-32): Work in stockinette stitch, starting with a k row.
Work short rows.
Row 31 (31, 33): K18 (19, 21), k2tog, k17 (19, 19), k2tog, turn. 55 (59, 63) sts.
Row 32 (32, 34): Sl1, p17 (19, 19), p2tog, turn. 54 (58, 62).
Row 33 (33, 35): Sl1, k17 (19, 19), k2tog, turn. 53 (57, 61) sts.
Rows 34-53 (34-55, 36-61): Rep. last 2 rows 10 (11, 13) times. 33 (35, 35) sts.

Row 54 (56, 62): Rep. row 32 (32, 34) once. 32 (34, 34) sts.
Row 55 (57, 63): Sl1, [p1, k1] 8 (9, 9) times, p1, k2tog, turn. 31 (33, 33) sts.
Row 56 (58, 64): Sl1, [k1, p1] 8 (9, 9) times, k1, p2tog, turn. 30 (32, 32) sts.
Rows 57-66 (59-68, 65-74): Rep. last 2 rows 5 (5, 5) times. 20 (22, 22) sts.

NECK RUFF

Work in the round with US 8 (5mm) circular needles.
Round 67 (69, 75): Sl1, [p1, k1] 8 (9, 9) times, p1, k2tog, pick up and knit 13 (12, 12) sts along edge, cast on 7 sts, pick up and knit 13 (12, 12) sts along edge. 52 (52, 52) sts.
Rounds 68-77 (70-81, 76-89): Work in k1, p1, rib.
Round 78 (82, 90): K2 (3, 3), [yo, k2, yo, k11] 3 (3, 3) times, yo, k2, yo, k9 (8, 8). 60 (60, 60) sts.
Round 79 (83, 91): K3 (4, 4), [yo, k2, yo, k13] 3 (3, 3) times, yo, k2, yo, k10 (9, 9). 68 (68, 68) sts.
Round 80 (84, 92): K4 (5, 5), [yo, k2, yo, k15 (15, 15)] 3 (3, 3) times, yo, k2, yo, k11 (10, 10). 76 (76, 76) sts.
Round 81 (85, 93): K5 (6, 6), [yo, k2, yo, k17 (17, 17)] 3 (3, 3) times, yo, k2, yo, k12 (11, 11). 84 (84, 84) sts.
Round 82 (86, 94): K6 (7, 7), [yo, k2, yo, k19 (19, 19)] 3 (3, 3) times, yo, k2, yo, k13 (12, 12). 92 (92, 92) sts.
Round 83 (87, 95): K7 (8, 8), yo, [k2, k21 (21, 21)] 3 (3, 3) times yo, k2, yo, k14 (13, 13). 100 (100, 100) sts.

Use this photo as a guide to position the ear and horns on the back of the hat.

12-24 months and 2-3 years:

Round (88, 96): K (9, 9), [yo, k2, yo, k (23, 23)] 3 (3, 3) times, yo, k2, yo, k (14, 14). (108, 108) sts.
Round (89, 97): K (10, 10), [yo, k2, yo, k (25, 25)] 3 (3, 3) times, yo, k2, yo, k (15, 15). (116, 116) sts.

2-3 years:

Round (98): K11, [yo, k2, yo, k27] 3 (3, 3) times, yo, k2, yo, k16. 124 sts.
Round (99): K12, [yo, k2, yo, k29] 3 (3, 3) times, yo, k2, yo, k17. 132 sts.

All sizes:

Rounds 84-89 (90-95, 100-105):
Work in k1, p1, rib.
Bind off.

This photo indicates the positioning of the features at the front of the hat.

NOSE

With US G-6 (4.25mm) crochet hook and yarn B: Ch4. Join with sl st to form ring.
Work in a spiral. Don't join at the end of a row but continue working.
Round 1: 7sc into the center of ring.
Round 2: 2sc into each sc. 14sc.
Round 3: 1 sc into each sc. 14sc.
Round 4: 1 sc into each sc. 14sc.
End with sl st in next st to join.
Fasten off.

NOSTRILS
(make 2)

With US G-6 (4.25mm) crochet hook and yarn B: Ch4. Join with sl st to form a ring.
Round 1: 6sc into the center of ring.
Round 2: 6sc into each sc. 36sc
Join with sl st to the first st.
Fasten off.

HORNS
(make 2)

With US 8 (5mm) double-pointed needles and yarn B, cast on 10 sts.
Join to work in the round.
Rounds 1-8: Knit.

Shape small horn

Round 9: K1, m1, k9. 11 sts.
Round 10 and each alt round: Knit.
Round 11: K1, m1, k1, m1, k9. 13 sts.
Round 13: K1, m1, k3, m1, k9. 15 sts.
Round 15: K1, m1, k5, m1, k9. 17 sts.
Round 17: K1, place next 7 sts on waste yarn. Rejoin to work horn stitches in the round, k9. 10 sts.
Rounds 18-23: Knit.
Round 24: [K2tog] to end of round. 5 sts.
Cut yarn, thread through remaining stitches, and draw tight.

SMALL HORN
Transfer 7 stitches from waste yarn onto needles. Rejoin yarn B and pick up and knit 1 st in the corner where the horn meets the small horn. 8 sts.

Rounds 1-5: Knit.
Cut yarn, thread through remaining stitches, and draw tight.

EARS
(make 2)
With US G-6 (4.25mm) crochet hook and yarn B: Ch9.

Row 1: 1dc into the third ch from hook, 1dc in each of next 5 ch, 8dc in last ch, (turn work so you are working on bottom of chain), 1dc in each of next 7 ch, turn. 21 dc.
Row 2: Ch1, 1sc in each of next 7 sts, 2sc in each of next 3 sts, work into the next st [1sc and 1hdc], work into the next st [1hdc and 1sc], 2sc into each of next 3 sts, 1sc in each of next 6 sts. 30sts.
Fasten off.

TEETH
(make 2)
With US G-6 (4.25mm) crochet hook and yarn C: Ch6.
Row 1: 1hdc into the third ch from hook, 1hdc into each of the next 3ch.
Fasten off.

EYES
Small pupils (make 2)
With the crochet hook and yarn D: Ch4. Join with sl st to form ring.
Round 1: 7sc into the center of ring. Join with sl st into the first stitch.
Fasten off.

Circles (make 2)
With the crochet hook and yarn E: Ch4. Join with sl st to form ring.
Round 1: Ch2, 13dc into the center of ring. 14dc. Join with sl st into top of beg-ch.
Fasten off.

Circles (make 2)
With the crochet hook and yarn D: Ch5. Join with sl st to form ring.
Round 1: Ch2 (count as first st), 13dc into the center of ring. 14dc. Join with sl st into the first stitch.

Round 2: Ch1, 2sc into each st. 28sc. Join with sl st into the first stitch.
Fasten off.

Circles (make 2)
With the crochet hook and yarn C: Ch5. Join with sl st to form ring.
Round 1: Ch2 (count as first st), 13dc into the center of ring. 14dc. Join with sl st into the first stitch.
Round 2: Ch2 (count as first st), 2dc into each ch. 28dc. Join with sl st into the first stitch.
Fasten off.

Finishing
1   Put together all pieces of the eye on top of each other in order of size, starting with the biggest.
2   With C, embroider two small pupils (highlights) in satin stitch.
3   Sew the eyes to the hat in the position shown using an invisible seam.
4   Lightly stuff the horns.
5   Sew the horns to the hat in the position shown using an invisible seam.
6   Sew the ears onto the hat.
7   Lightly stuff the nose.
8   Sew the nose and the nostrils to the hat.
9   Weave in ends.

MITTENS
(make 2)

CUFF

With US 8 (5mm) double-pointed needles and yarn A, cast on 22 (24, 26) sts. Join to work in the round.
Rounds 1-10 (1-12, 1-14): Work in k1, p1 rib.

THUMB GUSSET

Round 1: M1, knit to end of round. 23 (25, 27) sts.
Round 2: Knit.
Round 3: M1, k3, m1, k20 (22, 24). 25 (27, 29) sts.
Round 4: Knit.
Round 5: M1, k5, m1, k20 (22, 24). 27 (29, 31) sts.
Round 6: Knit.
Round 7: M1, k7, m1, k20 (22, 24). 29 (31, 33) sts.
Round 8: Knit.

12-24 months and 2-3 years:

Round (9, 9): M1, k9, m1, k (22, 24). (33, 35) sts.

All sizes

Round 9 (10, 10): K1, place 7 (9, 9) thumb stitches on waste yarn. Rejoin to work hand stitches in the round, k21 (23, 25). 22 (24, 26) sts.

HAND

Rounds 10-17 (11-21, 11-23): Knit. Fasten off yarn A. Join in yarn C.
Rounds 18-19 (22-23, 24-25): Knit.
Fasten off yarn C. Join in yarn D.
Rounds 20-21 (24-25, 26-27): Knit.
Fasten off yarn D. Join in yarn E.
Round 22 (26, 28): Knit.
Round 23 (27, 29): [K2tog] to end of round. 11 (12, 13) sts.
Fasten off yarn E. Join in yarn D.
Round 24 (28, 30): Knit.
Round 25 (29, 31): [K2tog] 5 (6, 6) times, K1 (0, 1). 6 (6, 7) sts.
Cut yarn, thread through remaining stitches, and draw tight.

THUMB

Transfer 7 (9, 9) stitches from waste yarn onto needles. Rejoin yarn A and pick up and knit 1 st. 8 (10, 10) sts.
Rounds 1-6 (1-6, 1-8): Knit.
Round 7 (7, 9): [K2tog] to end of round. 4 (5, 5) sts.
Finish as for mitten Hand.

Finishing

1 With C embroider two small pupils (highlights) in satin stitch.
2 Weave in ends.

The striking mittens have eyes to match the head with tiny pupils embroidered in satin stitch.

garden gnome

This pointy little hat will turn any small child into the perfect gnome. The project is a little more complicated than the others but well worth the special effort. Unique pointed mittens complete the set.

Coverall hat and mittens

LEVEL: advanced

SIZES
6-12 months (12-24 months, 2-3 years)

Finished measurements
From "cheek to cheek" around the hat: 16 (16½, 17)in (40.5 [42, 43]cm)
Mitten circumference: 5¾ (6, 6¾)in (14.5 [15, 17]cm)
Mitten length: 5½ (5¾, 7½)in (14 [14.5, 19]cm)

Gauge
17 sts and 24 rows = 4in(10cm) square in stockinette stitch worked with US 8 (5mm) needles
19 sts and 24 rows = 4in (10cm) square in k1, p1 rib unstretched, worked with US 8 (5mm) needles

Materials

HAT

Yarn:
Color A: 1 x 3oz (85g) ball (135yd/123m) Lion Brand Jiffy Yarn, 100% acrylic, Apple Green
Color B: 1 x 3oz (85g) ball (135yd/123m) Lion Brand Jiffy Yarn, 100% acrylic, True Red

Equipment:
- US 8 (5mm) circular needles
- Optional: Stitch marker to indicate the start of a round
- Yarn needle

MITTENS

Yarn:
Color A: 1 x 3oz (85g) ball (135yd/123m) Lion Brand Jiffy Yarn, 100% acrylic, Apple Green
Color B: 1 x 3oz (85g) ball (135yd/123m) Lion Brand Jiffy Yarn, 100% acrylic, True Red

Equipment:
- 4 x US 8 (5mm) double-pointed needles
- Optional: Stitch marker to indicate the start of a round
- Stitch holder
- Yarn needle

HAT

With a US 8 (5mm) circular needle and yarn A, cast on 110 (120, 140) sts. Join to work in the round.

NECK RUFF

6-12 months:
Round 1: [K1, p4, k1, p5] 10 times. 110 sts.

12-24 months:
Round 1: [K1, p5] 20 times. 120 sts.
Round 2: Knit.
Round 3: [K1, p2, p2tog, p1, k1, p5] 10 times. 110 sts.

2-3 years:
Round 1: [K1, p6] 20 times. (140) sts.
Round 2: Knit.
Round 3: [K1, p2, p2tog, p2, k1, p6] 10 times. (130) sts.
Round 4: Knit.

Round 5: [K1, p5, k1, p2, p2tog, p2] 10 times. (120) sts.
Round 6: Knit.
Round 7: [K1, p2, p2tog, p1, k1, p5] 10 times. 110 sts.

All sizes:

Note: For the remainder of the Neck ruff, the pattern copy and the total number of stitches at the end of each round are the same for each size.
Round 2 (4, 8): Knit.
Round 3 (5, 9): [K1, p4, k1, p2, p2tog, p1] 10 times. 100 sts.
Round 4 (6, 10): Knit.
Round 5 (7, 11): [K1, p1, p2tog, p1, k1, p4] 10 times. 90 sts.
Round 6 (8, 12): Knit.
Round 7 (9, 13): [K1, p3, k1, p1, p2tog, p1] 10 times. 80 sts.
Round 8 (10, 14): Knit.
Round 9 (11, 15): [K1, p1, p2tog, k1, p3] 10 times. 70 sts.

Round 10 (12, 16): Knit.
Round 11 (13, 17): [K1, p2, k1, p1, p2tog] 10 times. 60 sts.
Round 12 (14, 18): Knit.
Round 13 (15, 19): [K1, p2tog, k1, p2] 10 times. 50 sts.
Round 14 (16, 20): Knit.
Round 15 (17, 21): [K1, p1, k1, p2] 10 times. 50 sts.
Rounds 16-21 (18-25, 22-31): Rep. last 2 rounds. 50 sts.
Round 22 (26, 32): K6, [m1, k4] 4 times, bind off 6 sts, [k4, m1] 4 times, k6. 52 (52, 52) sts.
Fasten off yarn A. Join in yarn B.

HEAD

Round 23 (27, 33): K26, cast on 53 (55, 57) stitches. Rejoin to work in the round, k26. 105 (107, 109) sts.
Round 24 (28, 34): K25, k2tog, [p1, k1] 25 (26, 27) times, p1, k2tog, turn, sl1, [k1, p1] 25 (26, 27) times, k1, p2tog, turn, sl1, [p1, k1] 25 (26, 27) times, p1, k2tog, turn, sl1, [k1, p1] 25 (26, 27) times, k1, p2tog, turn, sl1, [p1, k1] 25 (26, 27) times, p1, k2tog, turn, sl1, [k1, p1] 25 (26, 27) times, k1, p2tog, turn, sl1, k51 (53, 55), k2tog, k22. 97 (99, 101) sts.
Round 25 (29, 35): K1, m1, k19, [k2tog] twice, k49 (51, 53), [k2tog] twice, k19, m1, k1. 95 (97, 99) sts.
Round 26 (30, 36): Knit.
Round 27 (31, 37): K20, [k2tog] twice, k47 (49, 51), [k2tog] twice, k20. 91 (93, 95) sts.

This pattern is necessarily complicated to achieve the classic cone shape that garden gnomes favor. It's well worth all your hard work!

Round 28 (32, 38): Knit.
Round 29 (33, 39): K19, [k2tog] twice, k45 (47, 49), [k2tog] twice, k19. 87 (89, 91) sts.
Round 30 (34, 40): Knit.
Round 31 (35, 41): K1, m1, k17, [k2tog] twice, k43 (45, 47), [k2tog] twice, k17, m1, k1. 85 (87, 89) sts.
Round 32 (36, 42): Knit.
Round 33 (37, 43): K18, [k2tog] twice, k41 (43, 45), [k2tog] twice, k18. 81 (83, 85) sts.
Round 34 (38, 44): Knit.
Round 35 (39, 45): K17, [k2tog] twice, k39 (41, 43), [k2tog] twice, k17. 77 (79, 81) sts.
Round 36 (40, 46): Knit.
Round 37 (41, 47): K1, m1, k15, [k2tog] twice, k37 (39, 41), [k2tog] twice, k15, m1, k1. 75 (77, 79) sts.
Round 38 (42, 48): Knit.
Round 39 (43, 49): K16, [k2tog] twice, k35 (37, 39), [k2tog] twice, k16. 71 (73, 75) sts.
Round 40 (44, 50): Knit.
Round 41 (45, 51): K15, [k2tog] twice, k33 (35, 37), [k2tog] twice, k15. 67 (69, 71) sts.
Round 42 (46, 52): Knit.
Round 43 (47, 53): K1, m1, k13, [k2tog] twice, k31 (33, 35), [k2tog] twice, k13, m1, k1. 65 (67, 69) sts.
Round 44 (48, 54): Knit.
Round 45 (49, 55): K14, [k2tog] twice, k29 (31, 33), [k2tog] twice, k14. 61 (63, 65) sts.
Round 46 (50, 56): Knit.
Round 47 (51, 57): K13, [k2tog] twice, k27 (29, 31), [k2tog] twice, k13. 57 (59, 61) sts.
Round 48 (52, 58): Knit.

6-12 months:
Round 49: K12, [k2tog] twice, k25, [k2tog] twice, k12, m1. 54 sts.

Round 50: Knit.
Round 51: K11, [k2tog] twice, k23, [k2tog] twice, k12. 50 sts.
Round 52: Knit.
Round 53: K10, [k2tog] twice, k21, [k2tog] twice, k11. 46 sts.
Round 54: Knit.
Round 55: K9, [k2tog] twice, k19, [k2tog] twice, k10. 42 sts.
Round 56: Knit.
Round 57: K8, [k2tog] twice, k17, [k2tog] twice, k9. 38 sts.

12-24 months and 2-3 years:
Round (53, 59): K1, m1, k11, [k2tog] twice, k (27, 29), [k2tog] twice, k11, m1, k1. (57, 59) sts.
Round (54, 60): Knit.
Round (55, 61): K12, [k2tog] twice, k (25, 27), [k2tog] twice, k12. (53, 55) sts.
Round (56, 62): Knit.
Round (57, 63): K11, [k2tog] twice, k (23, 25), [k2tog] twice, k11. (49, 51) sts.
Round (58, 64): Knit.

12-24 months:
Round 59: K10, [k2tog] twice, k21, [k2tog] twice, k10, m1. 46 sts.
Round 60: Knit.
Round 61: K9, [k2tog] twice, k19, [k2tog] twice, k9. 42 sts.
Round 62: Knit.
Round 63: K8, [k2tog] twice, k17, [k2tog] twice, k9. 38 sts.

2-3 years:
Round 65: K1, m1, k9, [k2tog] twice, k23, [k2tog] twice, k9, m1, k1. 49 sts.
Round 66: Knit.
Round 67: K10, [k2tog] twice, k21, [k2tog] twice, k10. 45 sts.
Round 68: Knit.

Round 69: K9, [k2tog] twice, k19, [k2tog] twice, k9. 41 sts.
Round 70: Knit.
Round 71: K8, [k2tog] twice, k17, [k2tog] twice, k8, m1. 38 sts.

All sizes
Note: For the remainder of the Head, the pattern copy and the total number of stitches at the end of each round are the same for each size.
Round 58 (64, 72): Knit.
Round 59 (65, 73): K7, [k2tog] twice, k15, [k2tog] twice, k8. 34 sts.
Round 60 (66, 74): Knit.
Round 61 (67, 75): K6, [k2tog] twice, k13, [k2tog] twice, k7. 30 sts.
Round 62 (68, 76): Knit.
Round 63 (69, 77): K5, [k2tog] twice, k11, [k2tog] twice, k6. 26 sts.
Round 64 (70, 78): Knit.
Round 65 (71, 79): K4, k2tog twice, k9, [k2tog] twice, k5. 22 sts.
Round 66 (72, 80): Knit.
Round 67 (73, 81): K3, [k2tog] twice, k7, [k2tog] twice, k4. 18 sts.
Round 68 (74, 82): Knit.
Round 69 (75, 83): K2, [k2tog] twice, k5, [k2tog] twice, k3. 14 sts.
Round 70 (76, 84): Knit.
Round 71 (77, 85): K1, [k2tog] twice, k3, [k2tog] twice, k2. 10 sts.
Round 72 (78, 86): Knit.
Round 73 (79, 87): [k2tog] twice, k1, [k2tog] twice, k1. 6 sts.
Round 74 (80, 88): Knit.
Round 75 (81, 89): [K2tog] 3 times. 3 sts.
Cut yarn, thread through remaining stitches, and draw tight.

Finishing
Weave in ends.

MITTENS

6-12 months:
With US 8 (5mm) double-pointed needles and yarn A, cast on 45 sts. Join to work in the round.
Round 1: [K1, p4] 9 times. 45 sts.
Round 2and each alt round: Knit.
Round 3: [K1, p1, p2tog, p1, k1, p4] 4 times, k1, p1, p2tog, p1. 40 sts.
Round 5: [K1, p3, k1, p1, p2tog, p1] 4 times, k1, p3. 36 sts.
Round 7: [K1, p1, p2tog, k1, p3] 4 times, k1, p1, p2tog. 31 sts.
Round 9: [K1, p2, k1, p1, p2tog] 4 times, k1, p2. 27 sts.
Round 11: [K1, p2tog, k1, p2] 4 times, k1, p2tog. 22 sts.
Round 13: [K1, p1, k1, p2, k1, p1, k1, p2tog] twice, k1, p1. 20 sts.
Fasten off yarn A. Join in yarn B.
Rounds 14-19: Knit.

Right mitten:
Round 20: Place first 4 stitches onto waste yarn, cast on 4 stitches (right-hand needle), join to work in the round, k16. 20 sts.

Left mitten:
Round 20: K6, place next 4 stitches onto waste yarn, cast on 4 stitches (right-hand needle), join to work in the round, k10. 20 sts.

Both mittens:
Rounds 21-31: Knit.
Round 32: [K2tog, k6, k2tog] twice. 16 sts.
Round 33: [K2tog, k4, k2tog] twice. 12 sts.
Round 34: [K2tog, k2, k2tog] twice. 8 sts.
Round 35: [K2tog] to end of round. 4 sts.
Cut yarn, thread through remaining stitches, and draw tight.

THUMB
Transfer 4 stitches from waste yarn onto US 8 (5mm) needles, join in yarn B, pick up and knit 4 sts across the 4 cast-on sts. 8 sts. Join to work in the round.
Rounds 1-8: Knit.
Round 9: [K2tog] to end of round. 4 sts.
Finish as for mitten Hand.

12-24 months:
With US 8 (5mm) double-pointed needles and yarn A, cast on 49 sts. Join to work in the round.
Round 1: [K1, p4, k1, p5] 4 times, k1, p4. 49 sts.
Round 2 and each alt round: Knit.
Round 3: [K1, p4, k1, p2, p2tog, p1] 4 times, k1, p4. 45 sts.
Round 5: [K1, p1, p2tog, p1, k1, p4] 4 times, k1, p1, p2tog, p1. 40 sts.
Round 7: [K1, p3, k1, p1, p2tog, p1] 4 times, k1, p3. 36 sts.
Round 9: [K1, p1, p2tog, k1, p3] 4 times, k1, p1, p2tog. 31 sts.
Round 11: [K1, p2, k1, p1, p2tog] 4 times, k1, p2. 27 sts.
Round 13: [K1, p2tog, k1, p2]

4 times, k1, p2tog. 22 sts.
Fasten off yarn A. Join in yarn B.
Rounds 14-21: Knit.

Right mitten:
Round 22: Place first 5 stitches onto waste yarn, cast on 5 stitches (right-hand needle), join to work in the round, k17. 22 sts.

Left mitten:
Round 22: K6, place next 5 stitches onto waste yarn, cast on 5 stitches (right-hand needle), join to work in the round, k11. 22 sts.

Both mittens:
Rounds 23-34: Knit.
Round 35: [K2tog, k7, k2tog] twice. 18 sts.
Round 36: [K2tog, k5, k2tog] twice. 14 sts.
Round 37: [K2tog, k3, k2tog] twice. 10 sts.
Round 38: [K2tog, k1, k2tog] twice. 6 sts.
Cut yarn, thread through remaining stitches, and draw tight.

THUMB
Transfer 5 stitches from waste yarn onto needles, using yarn B, pick up and knit 5 sts across the 5 cast-on sts. 10 sts.
Join to work in the round.
Rounds 1-9: Knit.
Round 10: [K2tog, k1, k2tog] twice. 6 sts.
Finish as for mitten Hand.

2-3 years:
With US 8 (5mm) double-pointed needles and A, cast on 54 sts. Join to work in the round.
Round 1: [K1, p5] 9 times. 54 sts.

The garden gnome mittens are truly original with their pointed tops and flared cuffs.

Round 2 and each alt round: Knit.
Round 3: [K1, p2, p2tog, p1, k1, p5] 4 times, k1, p2, p2tog, p1. 49 sts.
Round 5: [K1, p4, k1, p2, p2tog, p1] 4 times, k1, p4. 45 sts.
Round 7: [K1, p1, p2tog, p1, k1, p4] 4 times, k1, p1, p2tog, p1. 40 sts.
Round 9: [K1, p3, k1, p1, p2tog, p1] 4 times, k1, p3. 36 sts.
Round 11: [K1, p1, p2tog, k1, p3] 4 times, k1, p1, p2tog. 31 sts.
Round 13: [K1, p2, k1, p1, p2tog] 4 times, k1, p2. 27 sts.
Fasten off yarn A. Join in yarn B.
Rounds 14-23: Knit.

Right mitten:
Round 24: Place first 5 stitches onto waste yarn, cast on 5 stitches (right-hand needle), join to work in the round, k20, k2tog. 26 sts.

Left mitten:
Round 24: K8, place next 5 stitches onto waste yarn, cast on 5 stitches (right-hand needle), join to work in the round, k12, k2tog. 26 sts.

Both mittens:
Rounds 25-38: Knit.
Round 39: [K2tog, k9, k2tog] twice. 22 sts.
Round 40: [K2tog, k7, k2tog] twice. 18 sts.
Round 41: [K2tog, k5, k2tog] twice. 14 sts.
Round 42: [K2tog, k3, k2tog] twice. 10 sts.
Round 43: [K2tog, k1, k2tog] twice. 6 sts.
Cut yarn, thread through remaining stitches, and draw tight.

THUMB
Transfer 5 stitches from waste yarn onto needles, using yarn B, pick up and knit 5 sts across the 5 cast-on sts. 10 sts.
Join to work in the round.
Rounds 1-10: Knit.
Round 11: [K2tog, k1, k2tog] twice. 6 sts.
Finish as for mitten Hand.

Finishing
1 Weave in ends.

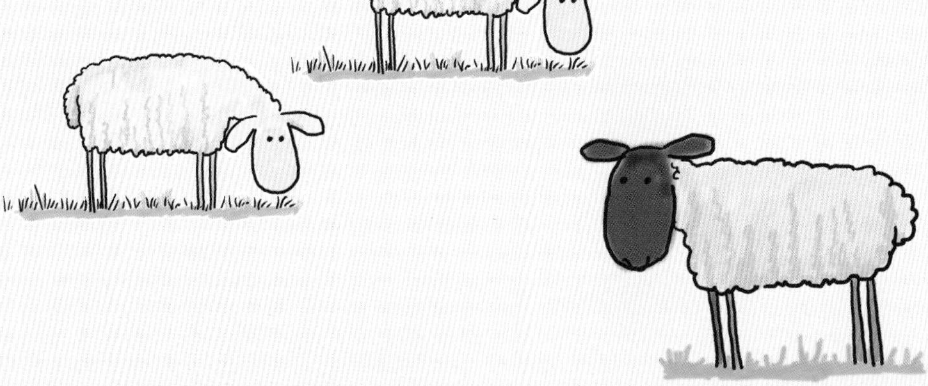

knitting
basics

before you start

equipment

Before you start knitting, gather together everything you will need for your project. For every *More Monster Knits* project, you will need the following:

- **Knitting needles:** check the type you need for each pattern (straight, double-pointed, or circular) and the sizes required
- **Small pair of sharp scissors**, used only for yarns
- **Needle gauge ruler or tape measure** for measuring the stitches and rows in the gauge swatch before you start knitting your project
- **Stitch marker:** when knitting in the round, you will need to mark the beginning of the round
- **Pen or pencil** for keeping track of where you are in the pattern
- **Yarn needle** for sewing up your project at the end

For some projects you will need:
- **Crochet hook:** check size required
- **Cable needle:** this is a short needle used to hold stitches temporarily while you are forming the cable

yarns

SELECTION

All the yarns in this book have been chosen because they are soft and comfortable to wear as well as being extremely warm. For the best results, it is best to purchase exactly the yarn stated in the pattern. Make sure that you buy enough wool for your project, and always check the shade and dye lot number on the ball band to ensure that each ball is the same color.

SUBSTITUTION

If you do need to substitute a yarn, always buy another yarn of the same weight as the one in the pattern. Knit swatches until you achieve the correct pattern gauge. You will need to figure out how much of the substitute yarn you will need. The patterns provide the amounts of yarn in both weight and length to help you to do this.

Note that if you select a different fiber, this can affect the design. It is best to stick to the yarns suggested in the patterns.

SIZING

The patterns in this book are written for three sizes: 6-12 months, 12-24 months, and 2-3 years. Coverall hats cover the entire head and part of the face, so the measurement given in the patterns is from cheek to cheek around the hat. To make sure you are knitting the right size, measure the circumference of your child's head from cheek to cheek at the widest point, just above the ears. To check mitten size, measure the circumference of the hand at the widest point, and the length of the hand. If your child is between sizes, it is best to knit the larger size.

abbreviations and conversions

KNITTING ABBREVIATIONS

cn cable needle

k knit

k2tog knit next two stitches together as one

M1 make one by inserting left-hand needle from front to back under the horizontal strand between the stitch just worked on the right-hand needle and the first stitch on the left-hand needle, and knitting into the back of the loop to form a new stitch on the right-hand needle.

p purl

p2tog purl next two stitches together as one

rep. repeat

sl slip next stitch onto the right-hand needle without knitting or purling

st(s) stitch(es)

yo yarn over

* * repeat directions between *** *** as many times as indicated

KNITTING NEEDLES

Metric	US	UK
2mm	0	14
2.25mm	1	13
2.75mm	2	12
3mm	-	11
3.25mm	3	10
3.5mm	4	-
3.75mm	5	9
4mm	6	8
4.5mm	7	7
5mm	8	6
5.5mm	9	5
6mm	10	4
6.5mm	10.5	3
7mm	10.5	2
7.5mm	11	1
8mm	13	0
10mm	15	000

CROCHET HOOKS

Metric	US	UK
2.25mm	B-1	13
2.75mm	C-2	12
3mm	-	11
3.25mm	D-3	10
3.5mm	E-4	-
3.75mm	F-5	9
4mm	G-6	8
4.5mm	7	7
5mm	H-8	6
5.5mm	I-9	5
6mm	J-10	4
6.5mm	K10.5	3
7mm	-	2
7.5mm	-	1
8mm	L-11	0
9mm	M/N-13	00
10mm	N/P-15	000

CROCHET ABBREVIATIONS

beg-ch beginning chain

ch chain stitch

dc double crochet

3dc three double crochets in same stitch

dtr double treble crochet

hdc half double crochet

sc single crochet

sl st slip stitch

skip2 skip two stitches

tr treble crochet

yo yarn over hook

reading patterns

If you are knitting patterns for the first time, take time to familiarize yourself with the abbreviations on page 119 and check that you can do all the stitches in the pattern. See pages 122 to 133 for explanations of the basic knitting techniques and pages 134 to 137 for crochet techniques. Details of basic sewing stitches are on pages 138 to 140. You may like to practice some of the stitches on a swatch before starting your project.

Note that the instructions are given for the smallest size first, with the two larger sizes in parentheses. Where two figures in parentheses are given, the row or round applies to the two larger sizes only. Where just one figure in parentheses appears, the row or round applies to the largest size alone. Before you start, it is advisable to photocopy the pattern and highlight the instructions for the size you are making.

Always check the actual size of the finished pattern before you start, and check the size will fit your child. You may like to adjust the pattern slightly; for example, if your child has long hands, you could knit a few more rows on the mittens.

smallest size first, with the two larger sizes in parentheses

make sure you have all measurements, equipment, and materials before you start

use the photos as a guide when making up the garment

unique unicorn

This fun mythical creature has a splendid horn that is stuffed to keep it upright. It's easy to create the appealing mane from lengths of gold-colored yarn. The matching mittens are created in the same main color.

Coverall hat and mittens

LEVEL: intermediate

SIZES
6-12 months (12-24 months)
253 (yards)

Finished measurements
From "cheek to cheek" around the hat: 14¼ (15¾) in (37 (38-29)cm)
Mitten circumference: 5½ (6-6)
in (14 (15-15)cm)
Mitten length: 5¼ (6½-7½) in (14-18.5-19)cm)

Gauge
14 sts and 19 rows = 4in (10cm) square in stockinette stitch worked with US 10 (6 mm) needles
16 sts and 19 rows = 4in (10cm) square in k2, sl1 rib slightly stretched, worked with US 10 (6mm) needles

Materials

HAT

Yarn:
Color A: 2 x 3.5oz (100g) balls 139yd/70.9m) Patons Classic Wool Roving Yarn, 100% pure new wool, Aran
Color B: Patons Classic Wool Roving Yarn, 100% pure new wool, Yellow

Small amount:
Color C: Patons Classic Wool Roving Yarn, 100% pure new wool, Natural

Equipment:
• US 10 (6 mm) circular needle
• 1 pair of US 10 (6 mm) double pointed needles
• US J-10 (6mm) crochet hook
• Optional: Stitch marker to indicate the start of a round
• Yarn needle
• Stuffing

MITTENS

Yarn:
Color A: 1 x 3.5oz (100g) ball (139yd/70.9m) Patons Classic Wool Roving Yarn, 100% pure new wool, Aran

Equipment:
• 4 x US 10 (6 mm) double pointed needles
• Optional: Stitch marker to indicate the start of a round
• Yarn needle

gauge

To achieve the correct size, it is important to knit to the gauge specified in the pattern. If the gauge is too loose, the garment will have an uneven shape, causing problems with the fit. If it is too tight, the fabric can become hard and inflexible. The gauge details for each pattern specify the gauge in both stockinette and rib stitch. Always make a sample to check the gauge before you start, using the correct yarn, needle size, and stitch pattern.

Knit a sample of at least 5in/13cm. Smooth it out on a flat surface, without stretching it. Mark 4in/10cm with pins and count the number of stitches between the pins. This is the stitch gauge. Then mark 4in/10cm vertically with pins, and count the number of rows. This is your row gauge. If you have more stitches and rows than indicated, the gauge is too tight. Knit a new sample using larger needles. If you have fewer stitches and rows, the gauge is too loose, and you should knit a new sample with smaller needles.

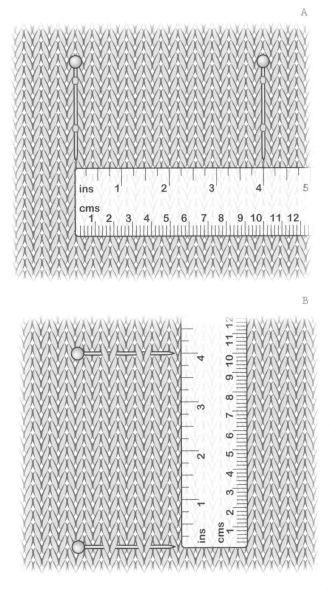

casting on

When you start knitting, the first step is to make a slip knot. Then you create a foundation row, known as a cast-on row. There are several ways of creating this row. Two of the most popular methods are described here: thumb cast on and cable cast on.

slip knot

1 Make a circle of yarn around the fingers of your left hand. Use the knitting needle to pull a loop of the yarn attached to the ball through the yarn circle.

2 Pull both ends of the yarn to make a tight knot on the knitting needle. This is a slip knot.

STEP 1

STEP 2

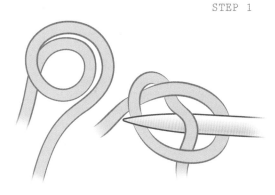

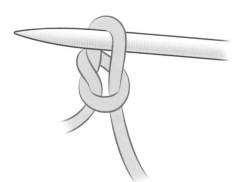

thumb cast on

This one-needle method gives a flexible edge with some give. Since you will be working toward the yarn end, ensure you have sufficient yarn for the cast-on row. Leave more yarn than you need; any excess can be used later for sewing up.

1 Make a slip knot (see opposite page), allowing a long tail. Hold the slip knot on the needle in your right hand and the yarn from the ball over your index finger. Wind the tail end of the yarn over your left thumb from front to back, securing the yarn in your palm.

2 Insert the knitting needle upward through the yarn loop on your left thumb.

3 Use the right index finger to wind the yarn from the ball over the knitting-needle point.

4 Bring the yarn through the loop on your thumb to make a stitch on the knitting needle. Allow the loop of yarn to slip off the left thumb. Pull the loose end to tighten the stitch. Repeat these steps until you have the correct number of stitches.

STEP 1

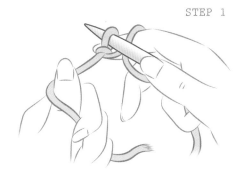

STEP 2

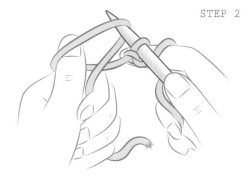

STEP 3

STEP 4

cable cast on

This two-needle method provides a strong yet flexible edge, and is excellent for ribbed edges.
It is one of the most popular cast-on methods. **Do not make the new stitches too tight**; you will need to insert the needle between them to make the next stitch.

1 Make a slip knot (see page 122). With the needle with the slip knot in the left hand, insert the other needle from right to left, and front to back, through the slip knot. Bring the yarn from the ball up and over the right-hand needle.

2 Using the right-hand needle, draw a loop through the slip stitch to create another stitch. Slip the new stitch onto the left-hand needle.

3 Insert the right-hand needle between the two stitches on the left-hand needle. Bring the yarn around the point of the right-hand needle.

4 Pull the yarn through to create a new stitch. Place the new stitch on the left-hand needle. Repeat steps 3 and 4 until you have cast on the correct number of stitches.

STEP 1

STEP 2

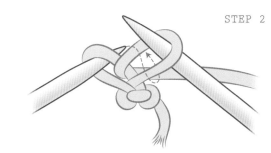

STEP 3

STEP 4

knitting techniques

knit stitch (k)

Knit stitch is the first stitch to learn. If you work knit stitch continuously, it forms garter stitch (see page 131).

1 Hold the needle with the cast-on stitches in your left hand. Insert the right-hand needle from right to left, front to back, through the first stitch.

2 Hold the yarn from the ball on your left-hand index finger. Bring this yarn around the point of the right-hand needle.

3 Bring the right-hand needle and yarn through the stitch to form a new stitch on the right-hand needle. Slip the original stitch off the left-hand needle.

Repeat these steps until you have worked all of the stitches on the left-hand needle. You have completed one knit row.

STEP 1

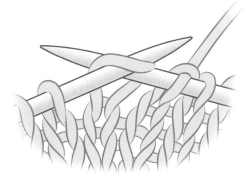

STEP 2

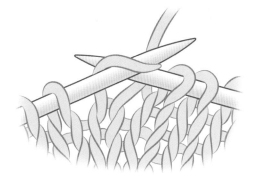

STEP 3

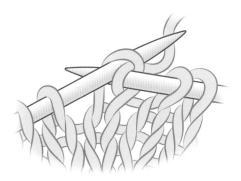

purl stitch (p)

Purl is the next stitch to learn. When knit and purl stitch are worked in alternate rows, they form stockinette stitch (see page 131), which is used for all the patterns in this book.

1 Hold the yarn in front of the right-hand needle. Insert the right-hand needle from right to left into the front of the first stitch on the left-hand needle.

2 Hold the yarn from the ball on your left-hand index finger. Bring this yarn around the point of the right-hand needle.

3 Bring the right-hand needle and yarn through the stitch to form a new stitch on the right-hand needle. Slip the original stitch off the left-hand needle.

Repeat these steps until you have worked all of the stitches on the left-hand needle. You have completed one purl row.

STEP 1

STEP 2

STEP 3

increase

You increase stitches to add width to the knitted fabric, for example, when creating the thumb gusset on the mittens. There are two ways to increase stitches in *More Monster Knits*; the patterns indicate which method to use.

MAKE ONE (M1)

1 Insert the left-hand needle from front to back below the horizontal strand of wool in between the stitch you have just worked on the right-hand needle and the first stitch on the left-hand needle.

2 Knit into the back of the loop. Drop the strand from the left-hand needle. You have created an additional stitch on the right-hand needle.

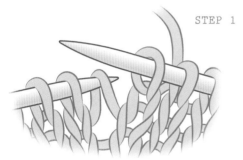

STEP 1

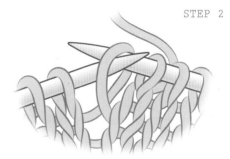

STEP 2

yarn over (yo)

1 YARN OVER BETWEEN KNIT STITCHES

Take the yarn forward between the needles, from the back to the front of your knitting. Take the yarn over the right-hand needle and knit the next stitch.

2 YARN OVER BETWEEN PURL STITCHES

Bring the yarn from the right-hand needle to the back, and between the needles to the front. Purl the next stitch.

3 YARN OVER BETWEEN A PURL AND A KNIT STITCH

Bring the yarn from the front over the right-needle to the back. Knit the next stitch.

4 YARN OVER BETWEEN A KNIT AND A PURL STITCH

Take the yarn forward between the needles from the back to the front of your knitting. Take the yarn over the top of the right-hand needle to the back. Then bring it forward between the needles. Purl the next stitch.

METHOD 1

METHOD 2

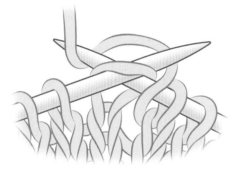

METHOD 3

METHOD 4

decrease

You decrease stitches to make the fabric narrower, for example, when shaping the bottom of a hat. There are two ways to decrease stitches in *More Monster Knits*; the patterns indicate which method to use.

1 KNIT TWO TOGETHER (K2TOG)

This is done on a knit row. Place the right-hand needle from right to left though the next two stitches on the left-hand needle. Knit them together. You have decreased by one stitch.

2 PURL TWO TOGETHER (P2TOG)

This is done on a purl row. Insert the right-hand needle from right to left through the next two stitches on the left-hand needle. Purl them together. You have decreased by one stitch.

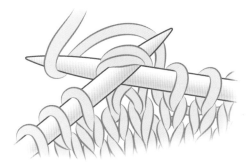

METHOD 1

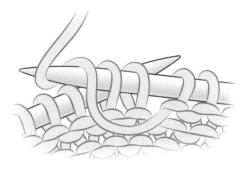

METHOD 2

bind off

Binding off is the last row of your knitting. Ensure that the bind off is firm but flexible so that hats, mittens, and booties can be easily pulled on and off. Always bind off in the pattern you are using.

KNIT BIND OFF

1 Knit two stitches as normal. Insert the left-hand needle into the first stitch you knitted on the right-hand needle and lift it over the second stitch, and off the needle.

2 You now have one stitch on the right-hand needle. Knit the next stitch. Repeat step 1 until you have bound off all of the stitches and have one stitch left on the needle. Pull the yarn through the last stitch to fasten off.

PURL BIND OFF

1 Purl two stitches as normal. Insert the left-hand needle into the back of the first stitch you knitted on the right-hand needle and lift it over the second stitch, and off the needle.

2 You now have one stitch on the right-hand needle. Purl the next stitch. Repeat step 1 until you have bound off all of the stitches and have one stitch left on the needle. Pull the yarn through the last stitch to fasten off.

KNIT BIND OFF

STEP 1

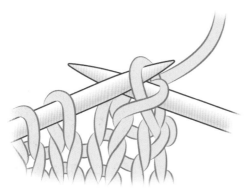

STEP 2

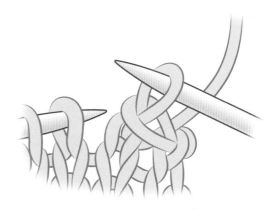

PURL BIND OFF

STEP 1

STEP 2

knitting stitches

STOCKINETTE STITCH
This is the most common pattern in *More Monster Knits*. To create stockinette stitch, knit alternate knit and purl rows. In this book, the knit side is the right side of the fabric.
Cast on the number of stitches required.
Row 1: Knit.
Row 2: Purl.
Repeats rows 1 and 2 to form stockinette stitch.

SINGLE RIB STITCH
More Monster Knits patterns use k1 p1 rib (single rib). You make the rib by alternating knit and purl stitches in the row, to create vertical columns of knit and purl stitches. The rib has an elastic · quality that makes it suitable for areas that need to stretch, such as mitten cuffs.
Cast on an even number of stitches.
Row 1: *K1, p1, repeat from * to end.
Repeat this row to form a single rib pattern.

DOUBLE RIB STITCH
A k2, p2 double rib is used to make the baby bear hat and mittens.
Cast on a multiple of 4 stitches and 2 more:
Row 1: K2, *p2, k2, repeat from * to end.
Row 2: P2, *k2, p2, repeat from * to end.
Repeat rows 1 and 2 to form double rib.

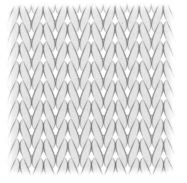

STOCKINETTE STITCH

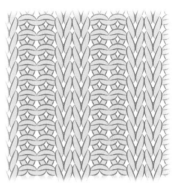

DOUBLE RIB STITCH

SINGLE RIB STITCH

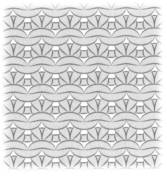

GARTER STITCH

GARTER STITCH
To make garter stitch, use knit stitch for all the rows.
Cast on the number of stitches required.
Row 1: Knit.
Repeat row 1 to form garter stitch.

SEED STITCH
Seed stitch is usually worked on an odd number of stitches.
Row 1: (right side): *K1, p1* end k1.
Row 2: Repeat row 1.

SEED STITCH

cables

To form a cable, you cross one set of stitches over another. The cable forms a vertical rope of stockinette stitch and makes an attractive pattern, for example, on the Polar Bear hat (see page 86).

BACK CROSS CABLE

1 Move the first two cable stitches purlwise from the left-hand needle onto the cable needle.

2 With the cable needle at the back of the knitting, knit the next two stitches on the left-hand needle. Make sure that you keep the yarn tight to prevent gaps. Knit the two stitches from the cable needle. You have made the cable cross.

STEP 1

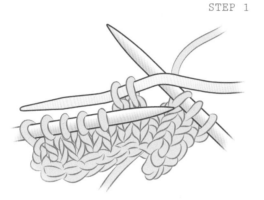

STEP 2

FRONT CROSS CABLE

1 Move the first two cable stitches purlwise from the left-hand needle onto the cable needle. With the cable needle at the front of the work, knit the next two stitches on the left-hand needle. Make sure that you keep the yarn tight to prevent gaps.

2 Knit the two stitches from the cable needle. You have made the cable cross.

STEP 1

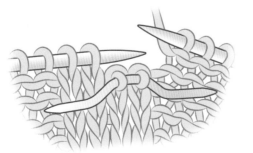

STEP 2

picking up stitches

When you are making the neck ruffs of a *More Monster Knits* hat, you will need to pick up stitches from the sides of the hat. The pattern will indicate how many stitches you need to pick up.

ALONG A SELVEDGE

Work with the right side of the knitting facing you. Insert the needle from front to back in between the first and the second stitches of the first row. Bring the yarn around the needle and pull a loop through to create a new stitch on the needle. Repeat along the edge of the knitting.

knitting in the round

For the patterns in this book, four needles are used to knit in the round. Divide the stitches evenly over three needles to form a triangle. Before knitting, make sure that the cast-on edge is not twisted. Use a stitch marker to mark the beginning of the round.

Start knitting the stitches with the fourth needle. As each needle becomes free, use it to knit the stitches from the next needle. When transferring from one needle to the next, pull the yarn firmly; this prevents a run from forming.

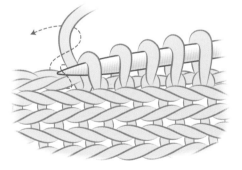

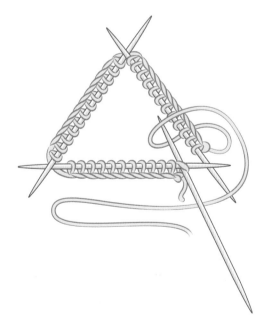

crochet techniques

crochet stitches

To make some of the *More Monster Knits* projects, you will need to be able to crochet. All the stitches you'll need are explained here.

Most people like to hold the crochet hook like a knife or pencil, but you can experiment to find out the most comfortable way.

SLIP KNOT
Every piece of crochet starts with a slip knot.

1 Make a loop in the yarn.

2 Use the hook to catch the ball end of the yarn. Draw it through the loop.

3 Pull on the yarn and hook to tighten the knot.

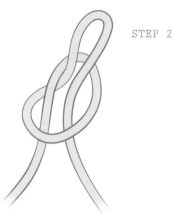

SLIP KNOT

STEP 2

MAKING A CHAIN (CH)
This is the foundation row of a piece of crochet; it is never counted as a row.

1 Make a slip knot, as above.

2 Hold the end of the yarn attached to the crochet hook with the left hand.

3 Pass the hook in front of the yarn, under, and around it.

4 Pull the hook and yarn through the loop formed by the slip knot.

5 Repeat steps 2 to 4 until you have the required number of chain stitches.

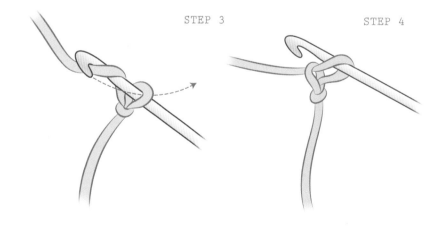

MAKING A CHAIN

STEP 3

STEP 4

SLIP STITCH (SL ST)

You need a slip stitch to join one stitch to another, usually to join a circle.

1 Insert the hook into the loops of the next stitch. (If you are joining the starting chain, as here, just insert the hook into the back loop.)

2 Pass the yarn over the hook (yo), as for the chain stitch and draw it through both stitches.

Slip stitch in a row

To make a slip stitch in a row, insert the hook through the two loops of the next stitch as below and follow step **2**.

STEP 1

STEP 2

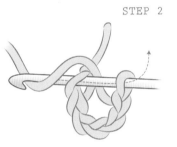

SINGLE CROCHET (SC)

This is a dense stitch commonly used in decorations for hats and mittens.

1 Insert the hook into the next stitch, front to back. Place the yarn over the hook (yo).

2 Draw the hook through one loop to the front, leaving two loops on the hook. Yo.

3 Draw the hook through the two remaining loops to finish the stitch.

STEP 1

STEP 3

DOUBLE CROCHET (DC)

Double crochet creates a more open stitch than single crochet.

1 Wrap the yarn over the hook (yo) from the front to the back.

2 Insert the hook into the next stitch, from the front to the back.

3 Yo. Draw through the stitch, leaving three loops on the hook.

4 Yo again. Pull through the first two loops.

5 Yo and draw through the last two loops.

HALF-DOUBLE CROCHET (HDC)

This stitch is half the height of a double crochet. In step 4, draw the hook through all the loops in one go.

STEP 1

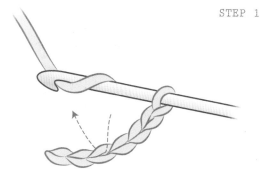

STEP 4

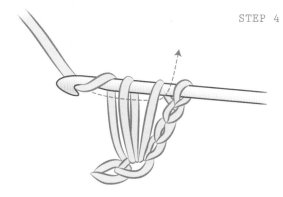

STEP 5

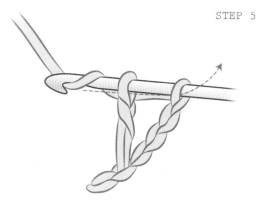

fastening crochet and weaving in

FASTENING OFF

1 Finish the last stitch.

2 Cut the yarn, leaving a tail of 2-3in/5-8cm.

3 Wrap the yarn over the hook, and pull the tail through the final loop on the hook.

4 Pull the tail tight to fasten the knot.

WEAVING IN

1 Thread the tail of the yarn into a yarn needle.

2 Thread the needle down the side of the work at the edge.

3 Pull the tail all the way through.

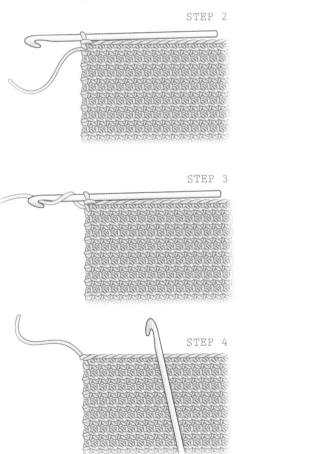

STEP 2

STEP 3

STEP 4

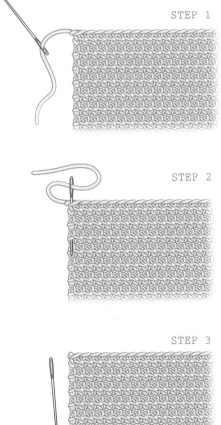

STEP 1

STEP 2

STEP 3

sewing stitches

Sewing up your project is an important stage of the job, which affects the look of the garment. When you cast on, it is wise to leave a long tail to use later for sewing up your project. If you have not done this, when you secure the thread for the seam, allow a length of yarn that you can darn in afterward.

The pattern instructions indicate when you should sew up the elements of the garment. In *More Monster Knits*, the grafting method is used to join up two bound-off edges. Always sew your seams with a blunt yarn or tapestry needle, which will not split and damage the yarn.

grafting

1 Butt the two bound-off edges together. Bring the needle out in the center of the first stitch, just below the bound-off edge on one piece. Put the needle through the middle of the first stitch on the second piece, and take it out through the middle of the next stitch.

2 Put the needle through the center of the first stitch of the first piece once again. Take it out through the center of the stitch next to it. Continue to sew in this way to end of the seam.

STEP 1

STEP 2

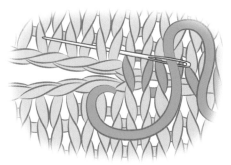

invisible seam

When you are making up your hat, you often need to join pieces with an invisible seam to achieve the best result.

1 Lay the two pieces next to each other. Insert the needle under the horizontal bar between the edge stitch and its neighbor.

2 Insert the needle under the parallel horizontal bar on the other piece. Work back and forth between the two pieces in the same way for a few rows.

3 Gently pull the yarn in the direction of the seam until the two pieces are together. Continue sewing until you reach the top of the pieces.

STEP 1

STEP 2

STEP 3

embroidery

The projects in this book use some basic embroidery stitches to sew parts of the project together. The yarn you need will be specified for each project. You'll also need a yarn needle.

STRAIGHT STITCH

Pass the needle in and out of the fabric. Make sure the surface stitches are the same length. The stitches underneath should be of equal length, but about half the size of the surface stitches.

STRAIGHT STITCH

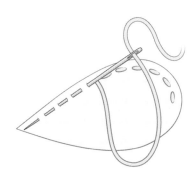

SATIN STITCH

1 Knot the embroidery thread and push the needle from the wrong side to the right side of the piece.

2 Push the needle under one stitch of knitting.

3 Pull out the needle, and make a stitch over the knitting, returning to the point where you started. Continue to make stitches in the same way to make the required shape, ensuring each one is right next to the previous one, with no space in between.

SATIN STITCH

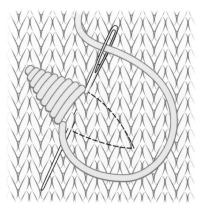

finishing and care

pompoms

Pompoms make delightful decorative details and are used on the Birthday Bear (page 76) and the Zany Zebra (page 38). Since these garments are for very young children, make sure to bind the pompom tightly so that little fingers cannot pull it apart.

1 Cut out two circles of cardboard the same size. They should be slightly smaller than the size of the pompom required. Cut a hole in the middle of each circle. Hold the circles together. Thread a darning needle with yarn. Wind it around the center and outer edges until you have closed the hole.

2 Insert a pair of small, sharp scissors in between the two cardboard circles and cut the wool between them.

3 Firmly tie a piece of yarn in the middle of the two cardboard circles. Remove the cardboard circles.

STEP 1

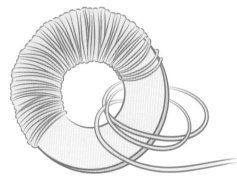

STEP 2

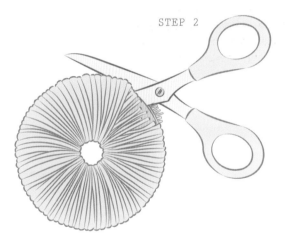

STEP 3

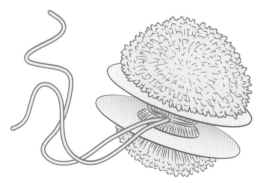

fringes

You will need this technique to make the mane for the Unique Unicorn (see page 98).

1 Cut the yarn strands so they are all a little over twice the length you would like the fringes to be.

2 Fold a yarn strand in the middle. Using a small crochet hook, insert the folded yarn into the piece you want to attach it to.

3 Use the hook to grab the yarn and pull it through the loop on the hook.

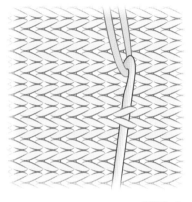

STEP 1

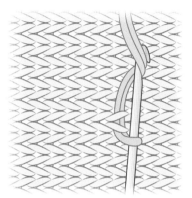

STEP 2

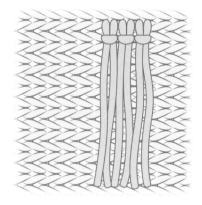

STEP 3

garment care

You will want to take care of your beautiful hand knits so that they last as long as possible. Bear in mind that garments for young children will have to be washed frequently, so it is important to follow the washing instructions carefully. All the yarns in this book are machine washable. Always check the ball band for washing instructions.

If you decide to hand wash your knits, ensure you use a mild detergent designed for knitwear, and warm rather than hot water. Immerse the garment in the water and squeeze it very gently to release the dirt. Avoid rubbing or agitating it. Once washed and rinsed, carefully squeeze out the water before taking it out of the bowl. Roll it in a towel to remove excess water.

Whether machine or hand washed, it is best to dry hand knits flat on a towel or other absorbent cloth. You can pat the garment back into shape while it is still damp. Never dry your hand knits on a radiator or other direct heat source.

index